UX PORTFOLIO DESIGN

IAN FENN

Chopstix Media Limited
149 Streatham Road
Mitcham CR4 2AG
United Kingdom

https://uxportfolio.design

UX PORTFOLIO DESIGN

ABOUT THIS BOOK

What this book is about

I've yet to meet a designer or researcher that enjoys putting a portfolio together. Most consider them a necessary evil and something to worry about only when a job search begins.

If I had the morals of a UX bootcamp organiser, I would promise that you will soon be able to create a UX portfolio painlessly. In reality, I hope you will learn how to make the process more efficient and less painful. Remember the old adage: no pain, no gain. I hope to explain how compiling your portfolio at the last minute is the worst thing you can do and how incorporating it into your regular work and design routine is the best.

Who should read this book

This book should interest anyone required to create a UX portfolio as part of the hiring process. This includes designers, research, design managers, content strategists, and UX copywriters.

Junior designers

It's hard when you're starting out. There are very few junior designer roles available and plenty of competition. Many junior design portfolios look the same. After reading this book, I hope you will be able to make your portfolio your own.

Senior designers

Creating a UX portfolio can be tricky for senior designers. We've passed through the 'novice', 'advanced beginner', 'competence', and 'proficiency' stages of the Dreyfus model.[1] We've arrived firmly in 'expertise' where our decisions are made intuitively, seemingly by magic. At times, it can feel like less-experienced practitioners are speaking another language. This book should help translate, so you can deliver what a less-experienced hiring manager will need.

Design managers

I've lost count of the number of design managers that have told me that they struggle with creating a UX portfolio because they are no longer involved directly in design work. This book ought to help you shift your perspective so that you recognise and document the amazing stories you have to tell.

Researchers

For some reason, a lot of researchers think a UX portfolio is a tool for designers that they are being shoe-horned into. That's a shame. In my experience, user researchers have the best stories to share. This book will show you how.

Content strategists and UX writers

The portfolios of content strategists and UX writers tend to focus a little more on the end result than other UX portfolios. However, this book will help you get the balance right against explaining how the work came about.

Product managers and others

If you fall into this category, the book will explain how to harness product design to ensure your portfolio is as effective and communicative as it can be.

---

[1] https://www.creativeacademic.uk/uploads/1/3/5/4/13542890/dreyfus-from_novice_to_mastery.pdf

How this book is organised

I've tried to organise this book in a logical way. Each chapter should logically follow the one before so it can be read in a linear fashion.

In Chapter 1, I provide a basic explanation of the UX portfolio, what works, and what doesn't. I also introduce the benefits of having one. It's not just a door opener.

Chapter 2 reveals the secret of reducing the pain in designing a UX portfolio. I'll cover how to take notes and the things you ought to pay attention to when working. I'll also explain how to approach previous projects completed before note-taking became a habit. (It will, right?)

Chapter 3 introduces the potential audiences for your portfolio and suggests a way of really understanding their needs. This chapter really ought to give you an idea of what to include for best effect.

Portfolio reviewers are often short of time. Chapter 4 explains design and writing considerations for an audience like this. Even if you are experience graphic designer or writer, I hope you will learn at least one thing new.

Chapter 5 discusses platform (pdf or web), format and also curation - which projects to choose.

Every portfolio starts with an introduction. I cover this in chapter 6, along with other biographical content.

Chapter 7 walks through the different components of a case study and introduces Highlights, which I believe are the hallmark of an effective UX portfolio.

Chapter 8 covers the remaining items you can include in a UX portfolio to further demonstrate your suitability to a hiring manager.

UX Portfolios are not without their challenges. I discuss these, including non-disclosure agreements, in Chapter 9.

The final chapter, 10, explains ways to quality-check your UX portfolio. I also explain the correct way to organise a portfolio critique session.

Need to produce a UX Portfolio quickly?

This is what I recommend:

1. Buy a third-party PDF portfolio template.[2] This will free you up to think about content rather than visual appearance.
2. Document your previous work in a spreadsheet as shown in Chapter 3.
3. Go through the job ad analysis exercise in Chapter 3 and Chapter 5. This will help you decide what to share in your portfolio.
4. Outline your case studies. Email me at ian@uxnotes.com for the Case Study Canvas.
5. Write your case studies and other content. (Chapters 6-8.)
6. Run your UX portfolio through basic checks and my checklist. (Chapter 10.)
7. Start maintaining a diary or logbook with my index method so that updating your UX Portfolio is more straightforward in future. (Chapter 2)

A note about the links

Any links referenced were correct when writing, but websites do come and go. If necessary, please try entering any rogue website addresses into the Wayback Machine at archive.org.

---

[2] https://gumroad.com/l/uxportfolio

A note about the portfolio examples

This book contains examples from publicly available portfolios. Sometimes, I share what I consider an excellent example of what not to do. I have removed names from these examples.

Please remember that these portfolio examples represent a moment in time. The portfolio has likely been updated since I captured it.

And if you recognise them and know the designers or researchers involved, please remember to be kind. We all make mistakes as we learn.

Thank you.

INTRODUCTION

You'll know you need a UX portfolio if you work in a UX or digital product role. Without one, you're unlikely to be able to find work. On the other hand, having a solid portfolio can deliver better job opportunities.

Since 2010, I've been researching the needs of hiring managers. I've reviewed thousands of UX portfolios for candidates. I've given talks and held workshops at popular conferences such as CanUX, Big Design, and South By Southwest.

Much of the published information about UX portfolios is subjective. Many authors share their personal opinion rather than proven evidence-based techniques.

This book is different. Based on my unique research with designers, hiring managers, and recruiters, I'll teach you how to create a strong UX portfolio that works for YOU.

I'm excited to be able to share this vital information.

1. THE UX PORTFOLIO: MUCH-MALIGNED & MISUNDERSTOOD

In this chapter, I plan to lay some ghosts to rest and address some elephants in the room. And use too many metaphors. I will leave no stone unturned.

Portfolio =/= portfolio presentation

Let's start with a necessary clarification. Your portfolio presentation and portfolio ought to be different documents.

When you present your portfolio, you're in the room or remote and can provide the narrative that accompanies it.

When you share your portfolio in advance, it's read alone without you, most likely by somebody who has never met you. It has to deliver the narrative in your absence.

For effectiveness, this requires two different but similar documents.

Portfolios are a conversation starter

For most companies, reviewing UX portfolios represents the first step in their recruitment process. No portfolio, no interview. Ineffective portfolio, no interview.

One way to look at it is this: The phone screen or being invited in to present your portfolio - that's the conversation. Sharing your portfolio in advance - that's a potential conversation starter.

Wrong tool or not, it doesn't matter

Occasionally, someone will write that the UX portfolio is the wrong tool. They could be correct, but it doesn't matter. Hiring managers far and wide have firmly decided: If you want an interview, share your portfolio.

Some senior UX practitioners have held on without a portfolio for a long time. I have bookmarked tweets from senior people years ago, declaring that they don't have a portfolio and never will. Today, those people have portfolios.

My occasional mentor Jared Spool has said that hiring managers should refrain from demanding a UX portfolio as the best designers may not have one. He's right, for now. But more and more designers have one, and as a candidate, do you want to be the one that doesn't? I suspect not.

A UX portfolio is a collection of stories

Let's say I left my home now and grabbed the first person I saw on the street. I could help that person create a UX-style portfolio. How? Quite easily.

A UX portfolio is just a collection of stories. Everyone has stories. Especially work stories.

Sometimes, Senior UX managers say, 'I can't do a portfolio. I don't do design directly anymore.'

If you're a lead designer or manager, your role means you have different stories.

Instead of design work, you talk about how you grew your team and facilitated their work. That's exciting stuff.

If there's one thing I want you to take away from this chapter, it's this: The secret of creating an effective UX portfolio is to use the skills you've been trained in or use every day.

Researcher? Discover the needs of hiring managers and deliver your findings!

Designer? Understand user needs and design what meets them!

Another critical point: You are not the primary user of your portfolio. Hiring managers and those involved in the hiring process are your users.

We'll discuss how to establish their needs in a later chapter. Let's now look at how you can benefit from a UX portfolio.

The next time you attend a networking event and a prospective boss or client asks you what you do, what will you say? Producing a UX portfolio means you have a bank of stories to share.

Mastering a skill takes not just time but reflection. Creating your portfolio will be easier if you maintain a work diary or logbook to draw from. So, start one. And now that you have one, use it for reflection. Think about your work. Reflect on your craft. Develop your skills.

Regularly update your UX portfolio throughout your career, not just when job hunting.

Over time, you may see patterns appear in your work preference. You may also observe gaps in skills and knowledge. Use this information to inform your future employment and training decisions.

UX portfolios also clear up confusion. My mate Dave, a UX designer, agreed to meet a prospective client. He spent an hour presenting his previous work. At the very end, he was asked, 'OK, but where are all the pretty designs?

Don't be like Dave. Send your portfolio as a pre-read in advance of meetings.

When the first interview is just a conversation, don't be surprised if your portfolio guides it.

When putting your portfolio together, ask yourself, 'What do I want hiring managers to ask me about?' And leave anything out that you don't.

A UX portfolio can be less critical if you're the type of person who can find work through people you already know.

But even in this situation, your pal can use your portfolio to justify your hire to the higher-ups. It'll help them explain your previous successes quickly.

Ever heard stories of how people found their work in other people's portfolios? I have. I dug deep, and in every case I saw, the plagiarist copied documents and UI designs. It's much more challenging to steal stories. So, focus on stories and make them your own.

What is the goal of your portfolio?

To get you an interview? Yes. But what does that mean?

A few years ago, my friend @cjforms tweeted that a user researcher's job is to help their team learn about users. Show how you did that.

If you're a designer or product manager, the goal is for your portfolio to show how you helped your team design the right thing and deliver it on time.

If you're a manager, your goal may be how you helped your team of researchers and designers help their teams. And how you helped the broader organisation to deliver better products.

There's a secondary goal.

You need to do more than show that you can do the job. You must also convince the portfolio reviewer they want to work with you.

So, two goals: 1.) To show you can do the job that the hiring manager is recruiting for, and 2.) to make them feel that they want to work with you.

The poorest-performing UX portfolios fail to meet these goals.

They're often collections of only high-fidelity screen mock-ups or UX deliverables. Even the old industrial design portfolio style of annotated products is insufficient. Stories are what you need.

There's a convention to portfolios now.

• An intro.

• Biographical content.

• Case studies.

• Then, additional content to provide a more rounded picture of the candidate.

Can you do something else? Sure, but there's risk involved. Whatever you do, be sure your approach considers user needs.

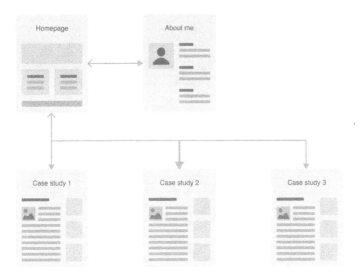

Figure 1.1 Most web-based portfolios are like this

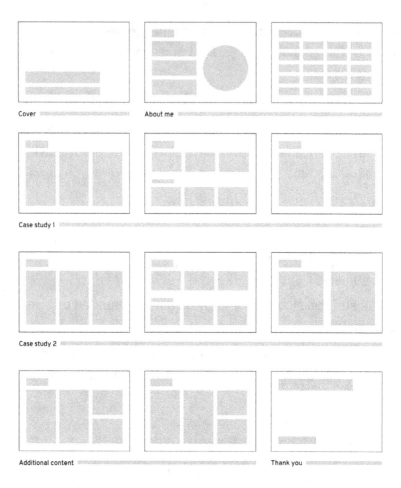

Figure 1.2 Most PDF portfolios look like this

2. CAPTURING YOUR STORIES

Many people assemble their portfolio at the last minute. Perhaps their work circumstances change, or they suddenly see a job they're interested in.

If you do this, you're likely to sell yourself short as you try to remember, weeks or months later, what you were thinking or why the project team took a particular decision.

The best portfolios are living documents and regularly updated as you work.

The key to building a UX portfolio easier is note-taking

Even if you choose not to maintain your portfolio regularly, keeping an organised work diary or logbook makes it far easier to find your stories when needed.

Note-taking is one of the most valuable skills a UX designer or researcher can perfect. It'll help your work and assist with portfolio production too.

Some designers use Evernote[3] or Day One[4] for their log book. Notion[5] is the new kid on the block. Maybe you have a Moleskine.[6]

I will take you through configuring a paper-based notebook, but I'm sure you can translate the instructions if you record your notes digitally.

---

[3] https://evernote.com/

[4] https://dayoneapp.com/

[5] https://www.notion.so/

[6] https://www.moleskine.com/

First, take a blank notebook. It can be lined, dotted, or squared. Whatever you prefer. Number the odd pages 1-15. Otherwise, leave them blank.

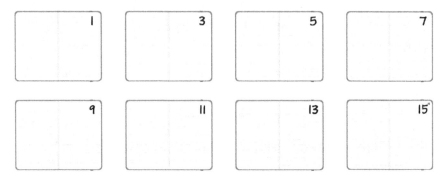

Figure 2.1 Number the first odd pages 1-15

That's the preparation done.

Next, start using your notebook as you would normally. But start with page 16. Number the odd pages as you go.

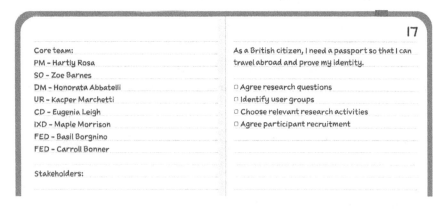

Figure 2.2 Start making notes from page 16

For example, for each project, you might record the following:

- The core team -- the people you will collaborate with on an everyday basis
- Stakeholders -- people with an interest in the project
- Goals -- the project's primary objectives, including success criteria or metrics
- Constraints -- any limitations or restrictions that you need to consider
- Users -- what you know about them
- Activities -- the tasks you and the project team will undertake to achieve the project goals
- Deliverables -- the documents you need to read or create
- You can also use your notebook to plan and record your day. Jot down:
- The three big things you want to achieve
- Your critical activities distributed across the hours of the day
- Then, write general notes as you go.

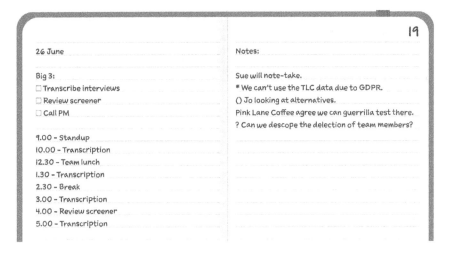

Figure 2.4 Carry on with your note-taking

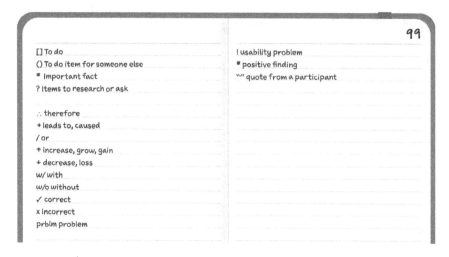

Figure 2.3 Some helpful abbreviations

Use abbreviations and shortcuts for to-do items, key facts and questions for quicker note-taking and easier reading.

What about those 16 pages we left blank at the start? That's your index. Put a project title at the top of each page.

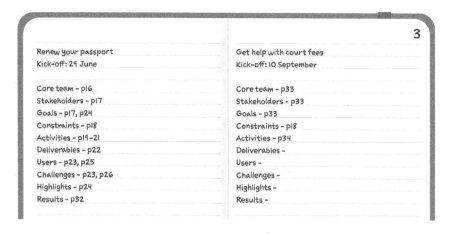

Figure 2.5 Use pages 1-15 as an index

Then, when you find yourself writing something in the main section that may be of significance to your portfolio, list it here with the corresponding page number. That way, you'll be able to find it again. There will be no more frantic reviewing of every page for a critical note.

You may wonder why we don't use the back of the notebook for this. It feels more natural to do it at the front.

I also use the rear of the book to keep quick reference material:

• Quick templates
• Reminders of what to do in certain circumstances.

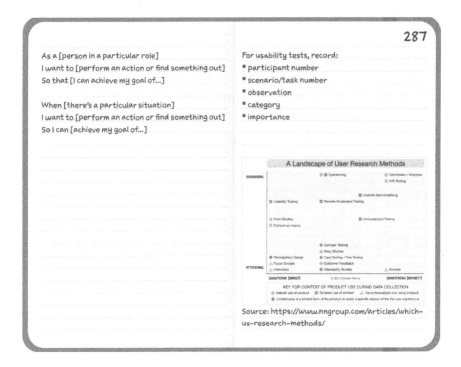

Figure 2.6 Use the back for reference material or gratitude

If you have the room, you can even glue in extracts from helpful diagrams or articles you want to hang onto.

One final thing about note-taking: be kind and give yourself enough time to write and review them.

For example, if you conduct six usability tests in a single day, they all blend into one another. Schedule 15 minutes after each session to review your notes and add further clarification where needed.

Photography

We almost all carry a camera around with us these days, so there's no excuse. Take photographs of everything.

OK, maybe not everything. But do ensure you capture the main activities and anything in particular that leads to an 'Aha!' moment.

Also, capture how you collaborate with other members of your team.

During field visits, take pictures that capture the overall environment. Office exteriors and interiors, for example.

Also, take mid-range photographs that show the research participant with other people and the objects they use.

Take close-up pictures of the participant interacting with specific objects.

Finally, for field visits. Capture close-up pictures of any objects that the participant uses.

Always seek permission from people to take photographs.

If permission is not forthcoming, try sketching. There's no need to produce works of art. All you need is a reminder.

During workshops, try to capture the overall workshop activity. Also, take photographs that illustrate a particular outcome, such as a single empathy diagram or a collection of related sticky notes.

Finally, capture close-up pictures of specific sticky notes and artefacts that are significant.

Figure 2.7 Curled Sticky Notes by You X Ventures on Unsplash

Photographing sticky notes

If you're taking photos of sticky notes, I have a few relevant tips.

1. It's annoying for sticky notes to fall off the wall. So, use good quality ones. When buying post-its, I always go for the 'Super Sticky' variant, and they rarely let me down.
2. If the sticky notes are sealed in cellophane-like plastic, squeezing the pad will break the seal and open them. It saves trying to find the irritating little end you need to pull to remove the wrapper.
3. Avoid peeling the sticky notes upwards and towards the adhesive strip. This will cause them to curl on the wall, as shown in this photo.

4. Instead, peel the sticky notes off sideways and parallel to the adhesive strip. You will get a flatter note.

5. Also, use a thick pen like a medium-fine Sharpie so what's written can be seen clearly and photographed well. Never use a ballpoint pen.

6. Write in capital letters so what's written is more legible.

7. Keep to a single point per sticky note so you can move notes around quickly and easily.

8. Finally, try to use colour meaningfully—one for requirements, another for features, for example.

Screengrabs

If you work on websites or software, frequently take screengrabs of your implemented designs. Capture the before state if there is one.

If you use third-party web-based tools licensed to your client or employer, you may lose access to them once you leave the project.

If your job contract allows, export copies of your work or if using an online prototyping tool like InVision, create a screencast video of the prototype in action.

Asset management

Now that you're collecting all this stuff, how will you store it? Let me share what I do.

When I start a project, I typically create a basic structure of empty folders within /clients/[client name]/[project name]:

/brief - what the client asked us to do

/content - text and images needed for the production of wireframes and full development

/design - site map, wireframes, prototypes

/research - documents related to research planning, execution, and results

This structure grows as the project progresses. I'll often add an archive to each of the above folders to store old files. I try to keep the names simple, consistent and meaningful (for me and others who need the files). For example:

/research/analytics

/research/site-crawl

/research/surveys

/research/usability-study

This approach has served me well for many years.

Dealing with historical projects

The chances are you've already undertaken some projects that you want to include in your portfolio -- this is where I suggest something I have nicknamed 'The Stockwell Spreadsheet' comes in.

The spreadsheet was developed by UX Research and Strategy Consultant Amanda Stockwell after she started to pull her portfolio together and found it hard to remember all of her previous projects.

The document contains a high-level record of the projects you have worked on, the work you undertook, and the results. Amanda told me:

"The idea came from a straightforward content inventory or audit. When you do a content audit of a traditional website, you write down what the pages are, what the URL is, what kind of page it is, and so on. I took that same approach to my projects. I wrote down the kind of project it was, my role on it, the timeframes, the decision points, and, most importantly, the results."

"I tried to find hard data that I could present as results to say, 'Look, here's where my impact was. Here's the difference that I made on each project.' For example, I worked on a large e-commerce project that made sales go up a certain amount."

Amanda suggests keeping the spreadsheet updated as you move through your career.

I prefer the logbook for tracking current work and see the spreadsheet as a valuable tool for providing a high-level overview of past work. At portfolio update time, you can review it to identify the projects to feature.

fx | Client

	A	B	C	D	E
1	Client	Project	Date	Tasks	Outcome
2	Three5		January 2014	Usability tests	Built out year long roadmap in under a week, internal clients very happy
3					
4	MPX	Usability Testing	January 2014	Usability tests	
5	MPX	Persona Creation	Dec 2013	Persona workshop	
6				Stakeholder interviews	
7				Survey	
8				Feature prioritization exercise	
9	Three5	Fl. Nav	Nov 2013	Stakeholder workshop	Updated navigation launched, conversion went up 20%
10				Survey	
11				User interviews	
12				Cardsort	
13				Wireframes	

Figure 2.8 The Stockwell Spreadsheet

29

A few people have kindly shared their portfolio spreadsheets publicly. Let's look at the one from UX consultant Eric Scheid.[7]

Note Eric's columns:

• The client or project

• The brief and challenge

• The result

• Timeline or duration

• Liaison/collaboration

• Activities and outputs

---

[7] https://twitter.com/ericscheid/status/1093716297102221313

ERIC SCHEID - UX PORTFOLIO - SELECTED CASE STUDIES

CLIENT / PROJECT	BRIEF & CHALLENGE	RESULT	TIMELINE	LIAISON / COLLABORATION	ACTIVITIES & OUTPUTS					
					DEFINE THE PROBLEM				DEFINE THE SOLUTION	
					Discovery	Analysis	Direction	Design	Prototyping	Testing
Commonwealth Bank commbank.com.au redesign	Complete redesign of public website to create new brand and responsive mobile first experience. Challenges: - very tight deadline - stepping in to replace original agency - no appetite for more research	289% increase in credit card applications within the first 30 days of launch. 305% increase in personal loan applications within the first 30 days of launch. 922% growth in transaction account applications within the first 30 days of launch. https://www.commbank.com.au/	3 months	Agency UX director UX team Development team	content inventory analytics review review CX task models	concept design concept testing	page templates global navigation site map principles	templates style guide sitemaps page outlines wireframes	user scenarios clickable prototypes	cognitive walkthroughs heuristic checklists client review
Starlight Foundation Children's charity website redesign	Full UX design for children's charity website to support new strategic direction. Challenges: - tight deadline and tighter budget - large client stakeholder contingent	10% reduction in bounce rate since relaunch & double the duration of user visits. 89% increase in donations month on month. "[they] took our new brand vision and showed us how amazing it could be, the designs were instantly loved by everyone that encountered them." https://starlight.org.au/	3 months	Client stakeholders Client project manager Agency designers UX team	analytics review donor surveys volunteer surveys competitor reviews stakeholder workshops	client card-sorts client workshop paper prototype tests affinity mapping	user personas client presentations client reviews	wireframes sitemaps site concepts	page sketches page templates	accessibility checklists navigation tree-testing usability test plans usability testing
SwiftPlan Media agency planning tool	Research & design new tool for marketing industry. Full project, from initial innovation research, concept design, through to launch. Challenges: - greenfield project - uncertain business model	"...I very well received with over 300 agency personnel already requesting user log-ins during our recent soft launch phase." "We built the original SwiftPlan to make planning letterbox media campaigns easier and more effective for our agency partners. We've had great feedback from our 2,000+ users." https://swiftplan.com.au/	3 months	Client product owner Business manager/ceo Agency designers	customer interviews competitor reviews contextual inquiries	concept sketches concept testing	concept designs story boards client review	wireframes user scenarios	clickable prototypes	cognitive walkthroughs heuristic checklists usability test plans usability testing
ACMA.gov.au ACMA's acma.gov.au redesign	Full website rebuild: - public facing information website - consumer registration experience - industry portal and tools Challenges: - tight deadline - minimal discovery research phase	Much improved navigation, easier content management, clearer distinction between consumer and industry sections, easier to find industry section. https://www.acma.gov.au/	4 months	Client stakeholders Agency stakeholders Agency designers Business analyst	content inventory stakeholder interviews analytics review	client style guide client workshops	user scenarios use cases client review	wireframes page flows sitemaps design patterns	clickable prototypes	navigation tree-testing cognitive walkthroughs heuristic checklists accessibility checklists usability test plans usability testing
Westpac Banking Online Transformation Project (Westpac Live)	UX design of multiple features of online banking experience. Challenges: - huge team - complex product - little budget for research	Much improved online banking site launched. https://banking.westpac.com.au/	11 months	Business analysts Product owners UX team	competitor review feature value survey concept media testing feature progress analysis page flows audit	feature prioritisation pattern design collection page flow reviews	design pattern library peer review/critiques stakeholder reviews	wireframes page flows sitemaps design pattern library	clickable prototypes	navigation tree-testing cognitive walkthroughs heuristic checklists

Figure 2.9 Eric Scheid's Spreadsheet

Here's another example, from Erica Heinz.[8]

Erica has listed the following:

• Whether or not a non-disclosure agreement applies

• Client

• Project name

• Challenge

• Timeline or project duration

• Design Process

• Methods used

• Result

• Any relevant URL.

It's almost a complete UX portfolio.

---

[8] https://twitter.com/ericaheinz/status/1024756132806582274

	CLIENT	PROJECT	CHALLENGE	TIMELINE	DESIGN PROCESS							RESULT	URL
					Research	Prototyping	Testing	Strategy	Visuals	Front-end	Back-end		
TOP 10 PROJECTS ▼▼▼▼▼▼▼▼													
Y	[big editorial site]	[new product]	identify opportunities for our future growth	4 months	in person user interviews	paper, wires, mocks, Principle, HTML	in person solution testing	collab w/agency	extend from current site	CSS animation demos	collab w/ dev firm	2-week strategy sprint extended to 20-week build	(alpha in development)
N	TurnTo	User-Generated Content Suite 5.0	satisfy our customers and help us lead the market	2 years	remote user interviews	mocks, Principle, HTML	remote usability testing	product strategy	extend from Material Design	collab w/ 3 Vue/Sass devs	handoff to client engineers	modular, themable, embeddable product	(in dev, login required)
N	ProPublica	Data Store 2.0	expand our single-page site into a capable storefront	5 weeks	competitive audits	wires	iteration w/client	content strategy	—	HTML + Sass + Jekyll	handoff to client; for design + dev	successful launch, still going strong	propublica.org/datastore
N	Hollaback!	HeartBot 1.0	prototype our idea for an anti abuse Twitter bot	4 weeks	—	digital mock	iteration w/client	product strategy	iterate marketing site	help on Sass	collab w/ 2 Rails devs	launched bot plus a support site	twitter.com/theheartbot
N	The B Team	event microsite	support Branson's project to redesign capitalism	3 weeks	—	—	—	tech + partnerships strategy	extend from agency branding	HTML + Sass	manage 1 WP dev	launched event site w/livestream, onboard, map, and no downtime	(temporary)
N	The High School for Community Leadership	marketing website	attract students, parents, and faculty to our mission	3 months	community surveys	—	—	content strategy	unique	HTML + Sass	manage 1 WP dev	"We look like a real school now!"	nychscl.org
N	CreativeMornings	Site 1.0	launch a site for our creative community	2 weeks	—	wires	iteration w/client	—	—	—	handoff to design + dev firm	organization grew from 1 to 180 cities (in 5 yrs)	creativemornings.com
N	Riffle	Riffle Books 1.0	develop a community of book lovers	2 years	remote user interviews, surveys	wires, mocks	remote usability testing	UX strategy	unique	HTML + Sass	collab w/ 3 Rails devs	product grew from 0 to 10,000 users (in 2 yrs)	rifflebooks.com
N	Sahana Foundation	LA Community Resilience Mapping Tool 1.0	help communities be prepared and capable in emergencies	2 months	remote user interviews	digital mocks	iteration w/client	—	minimum viable personality	CSS	Python	developed open-source skin for disaster relief tool	(login required)
N	Occupy Sandy	hurricane relief coordination site	assist grassroots disaster relief and recovery efforts	6 days	—	—	—	content strategy	minimum viable personality	HTML + CSS	collab w/ 1 WP dev	met deadline, gathered $1.6 million in donations	occupysandy.net

Figure 2.10 Erica Heinz's Spreadsheet

33

Doing good work

I love this quote from my friend Edward Tufte.

'Good design cannot rescue failed content.'

What does it mean in the context of UX portfolios?

It means no UX theatre. You must be doing user-centred research and design, not faking it.

While my research revealed that the needs of hiring managers could be highly individual, some elements of UX practice are more critical to UX portfolios than others.

There are certain things that many hiring managers will look out for. Let's go through them now.

Have a design process

First, if you're a designer, have a design process.

It could be the double diamond: discover, define, develop, deliver. Or perhaps the design squiggle - research and synthesis, concept/ prototype, design.

Whatever it is, make sure you have one.

Understand the business goal

Whether you're a researcher or designer, make sure you know the business reasons for your project. Simply documenting that you were asked to redesign the checkout flow isn't enough. Find out why. And if there isn't a formal brief, write your own.

Often the business goal is to increase profit, efficiency, or productivity. Perhaps it's one of these:

• Increase sales and market share

- Increase customer retention
- Ensure a product works effectively and efficiently
- Fix a product that the business knows is performing poorly
- Ensure a product delivers on time without scope creep
- Get a product to market quickly

The question "What's the one thing we must get right to make this project worth undertaking?" will often get you directly to the business requirements. A great follow-up is "What does success look like?" or "How will we know we have been successful?" Both questions should give you something to check the project against later on - and something to put in your portfolio.

Identify your users

Many portfolio reviewers will be checking to see if you know who your end users are. So, make sure you identify the following:

- who your users are (and aren't)
- the tasks that your users are trying to do and why
- any problems or context that would affect their ability to complete the tasks

Stakeholders may mention user needs, but they will only be aware of some of them. What they share may also be unwittingly influenced by their expert knowledge or a desire to meet personal business goals. So, there is no replacement for observing or talking with real users. Most portfolio reviewers will want to confirm that you have.

Sometimes we're denied access to users. Perhaps decision-makers are unconvinced of the benefit and cite a lack of budget or time. Maybe corporate policy or bureaucracy is too much of an obstacle.

If this is the case, do your best to obtain insight in other ways:

- Review existing analytics
- Examine support requests, emails, and social media posts by users
- Listen to support calls or interview support staff
- Buy relevant third-party research from organisations like Nielsen Norman Group[9] or Baymard Institute.[10]

Do what you can to understand user needs.

Know why you are using a specific tool or technique

As researchers and designers, we can use many different tools and methods. Be sure you understand why you're using each one as part of your process.

While there may be several options in a given scenario, portfolio reviewers expect you to have good reasons for your choice. It's not enough to say I'm doing personas because it's part of the user-centred design process.

Collaborate with others

Portfolio reviewers are rarely looking for people who work in isolation. They will want to know how you collaborated with others.

Of course, the amount of collaboration a company will allow will depend on its culture and organisation. But whether you facilitate regular workshops or pair design with colleagues, find ways to invite your colleagues into the design process.

There's an old saying: Great designers do not fall in love with their solution. Great designers fall in love with the problem. We know a lot about design, but it does not mean that other people can't have

---

[9] https://www.nngroup.com/reports/

[10] https://baymard.com/research

excellent ideas. So, lose the ego. Accept opinions from others and embrace critique. Respond with arguments, evidence or further thinking, not aggression or defensiveness. Reflect and ask questions. Never forget your ultimate goal: to help your team understand their users and solve a problem.

Throughout a project, actively listen to what people say. Listening allows those who need to talk through their thoughts to work things through. Others will feel a lot better once they have made their point. They'll relax and be more forthcoming about other issues. For the UX designer or researcher, being able to listen is a crucial skill.

If you work as a freelance or consultant, consider interviewing your client at the end of the project. Ask them:

• What benefits have you experienced from working with me?
• What specific results have you seen from implementing our solution?
• How successful was the project?
• What do you think I brought to the project?
• What surprised you about the project?
• What did you learn from the project that you did not know before?

As you close the interview with your client, ask if they would be willing to provide you with a LinkedIn testimonial.

Try a variation of this:

> "I would love to get a recommendation from you for my LinkedIn profile - I like to request this from key stakeholders at the end of all my projects. If I send you a request via LinkedIn, would you mind putting something together for me? Feel free to keep it brief."

3. UNDERSTANDING YOUR USERS

I've spoken with several hundred hiring managers and recruiters from across the globe over the past few years. There was one common complaint. They told me that 9 out of 10 of the portfolios they received were poorly curated with little focus or thought. They said they often work through irrelevant content to find what they want to see.

Very few people complete their UX portfolio with a clear understanding of their portfolio reviewer and their needs.

How can you uncover user needs? Well, the first step - like when researching or designing anything - is to decide who your users are. You will have difficulty putting your portfolio together if you skip this step. Analysis paralysis is likely.

Deciding who your users are

A UX portfolio is a sales document — in it, you're trying to communicate your value by showing how you delivered this on previous projects.

Few hiring managers review portfolios because they want to. They're doing it because they have to. The more you can do to make the task easier for them, the higher your chance of success.

The more you tailor your portfolio to the reviewer you want to impress, the more likely you'll be called for an interview.

• Who do you want to work for?

• Which companies will likely deliver the outcomes you want?

• Who will offer the culture and values where you feel like you belong?

Let's take a look at what corporates, startups, and agencies have to offer.

Corporates

First, the pros:

- You will often be able to follow and refine your design over time.
- You'll have relative job security, competitive salaries, and good benefits.
- Promotion prospects are also often better than at other companies.
- One final, significant plus: you're unlikely to be alone. There will be other UX people across the organisation to work with, learn from, commiserate and celebrate with.

The cons:

- There are exceptions, but corporates or larger companies tend to be risk-averse.
- So, they often have rigid processes and can be less interested in trying new techniques or ideas.
- The environment can be bureaucratic and highly political.
- Finally, seeing the results of your work can take a very long time because each stage must go through a lengthy approval and development process.

Startups

Pros:

- You can profoundly influence the product or service.
- Startups are experimental in nature, so they're open to trying new techniques or processes.
- They favour collaborative design.

- High financial rewards are sometimes possible, but employment is not without risk, given the number of startups that fail.

The cons:

- Your role is often to bring order to what would otherwise be chaos.
- You are likely the only researcher or designer, at least in the beginning
- Job security is far from guaranteed.
- Promotion prospects are limited.
- Finally, the hours can be extended.

Agencies

Agencies provide creative services to other companies. Roles can vary a lot, even if they have the same title. Some agencies specialise in UX design and have an unyielding focus on it. Others pay lip service to it. Most fall somewhere in between.

The pros:

- You'll be exposed to a variety of projects and problems.
- You'll have the opportunity to develop a broad range of UX skills.
- You'll also get considerable experience in client service and working with others.
- And if the agency is large enough, you'll have other UX people to work with, learn from, commiserate and celebrate with

The cons:

- Agencies need to satisfy clients. Decisions made to keep their customers happy may work against project goals. Also, payment from a client is often tied to the delivery of a document, such as a collection of personas or a report. Consequently, the design process may reflect what the agency needs to deliver for payment, not the project's actual needs.

- Agencies often win projects by participating in a pitch process where they present creative ideas that contain minimal or no user research. If the discovery process reveals that the client's users or customers need something different, it can be hard to get co-workers to let go of the original creative concept they loved so much.

- It's common for clients to have multiple agencies working for them on different but related projects. A single agency can therefore lack the ability to make changes to other work that fundamentally affects their own.

- Finally, projects are often short with the intention that the client takes over day-to-day operations following launch. Therefore, it can be challenging to see the project's result or to take steps to revise the design further.

Going freelance

If you have a few years of experience, going freelance is an option. Many UX designers choose this route as they can work on the projects they want rather than what an employer gives them. You can potentially make more than a salaried employee, but this comes with the risk of being unable to find work, at least occasionally. Depending on your work contract, you may leave projects before completion.

Along with the type of company you want to work for, you may also want to think about what you want to create.

You could specialise in software, hardware, websites, intranets and enterprise applications, web apps, or native mobile apps.

Alternatively, you could specialise in a particular company domain, although this is better done later in a career. Choices include finance, medical, pharmaceutical, gaming, retail, and government or non-profit. How do you choose from all these options?

Nathaniel Koloc, the CEO of recruiting consultancy ReWork, recommends that you think about the following:

- Legacy: This is about the concrete outcomes of your work. What do you want to achieve?
- Mastery: What strengths do you want to improve? For example, if you enjoy connecting with people, you could use that skill to be a psychologist or a marketer. The key is to use these strengths in a way you find rewarding.
- Freedom: This is about the salary, benefits, and flexibility you need to live the life you want. Ask yourself which job will help you fulfil the lifestyle that you want.
- Alignment: This last category covers your workplace culture and values. It is not about the company's mission but whether you feel like you belong.

Thinking about all these things, draw up a shortlist of the companies you believe will offer you meaningful work and ensure you feel fulfilled. Consider the portfolio reviewers at these companies the target audience or users of your portfolio.

Understanding the needs of hiring managers

Now that you have a shortlist of companies, it's time to uncover the needs of their portfolio reviewers.

Analysing job ads

We can uncover a company's stated needs by analysing job ads. You'll need a highlighter and any relevant job ads published recently by your favoured companies.

A good job ad will show 1.) what the applicant would need to accomplish in the role, and 2.) the expertise and skill set required,

A perfect ad would explain what success looks like for the candidate 90 days or even a year later.

Here's a typical advert for a product designer:

Responsibilities

- Take broad, conceptual ideas and turn them into something useful and valuable for our billion+ users
- Design flows and experiences that are incredibly simple and elegant
- Contribute to high-level strategic decisions with the rest of the product and executive teams
- Give and solicit feedback from other designers in order to continually raise our bar for quality
- Partner with PMs, engineers, researchers and content strategists to oversee the user experience of a product from conception until launch (and then some)

Minimum Qualifications

- Communication skills
- Demonstrated strategic product thinking and vision
- Experience in building and shipping applications or software
- Must have URL or case studies featuring examples of interaction design work
- Demonstrated experience with end-to-end (hybrid UX and UI) product design
- Ability to execute on visual and interaction details

Figure 3.1 A typical ad for a Product Designer

Using the highlighter, mark up anything significant like this:

Be sure to highlight the main tasks and any skills or personal qualities identified as required.

You should get something like this:

Responsibilities

- Take broad, conceptual ideas and turn them into something useful and valuable for our billion+ users
- Design flows and experiences that are incredibly simple and elegant
- Contribute to high-level strategic decisions with the rest of the product and executive teams
- Give and solicit feedback from other designers in order to continually raise our bar for quality
- Partner with PMs, engineers, researchers and content strategists to oversee the user experience of a product from conception until launch (and then some)

Minimum Qualifications

- Communication skills
- Demonstrated strategic product thinking and vision
- Experience in building and shipping applications or software
- Must have URL or case studies featuring examples of interaction design work
- Demonstrated experience with end-to-end (hybrid UX and UI) product design
- Ability to execute on visual and interaction details

Figure 3.2 The important stuff highlighted

Now, let's copy the highlighted information into another document.

I hope you will agree that this is much easier to deal with. You now know very clearly what this company is looking for.

But we're still not done.

Responsibilities

- Conceptual ideas into something useful and valuable for users
- Incredibly simple and elegant design flows and experiences
- Strategic decisions with product and executive team
- Give and solicit feedback from other designers
- Partner to oversee the user experience of a product from conception until launch

Minimum qualifications

- Communication skills
- Strategic product thinking and vision
- Building and shipping applications or software
- Examples of interaction design work
- End-to-end (hybrid UX and UI) product design
- Execute on visual and interaction details

Figure 3.3 Just the important stuff

Look for patterns.

For example, this product designer ad mentions decision-making with others, giving and receiving feedback, and partnering on user experience. Obviously, this company wants to see evidence of a high level of collaboration.

Also, this ad mentions interaction and user interface design skills three times. It's reasonable to think that this role leads heavily towards interaction and user interface design. So, it should probably be the emphasis of an applicant's portfolio.

Responsibilities	Minimum qualifications
• Conceptual ideas into something useful and valuable for users	• Communication skills
• Incredibly simple and elegant design flows and experiences	• Strategic product thinking and vision
• Strategic designs with product and executive team	• Building and shipping applications or software
• Give and solicit feedback from other designers	• Examples of interaction design work
• Partner to oversee the user experience of a product from conception until launch	• End-to-end (hybrid UX and UI) product design
	• Execute on visual and interaction details

Figure 3.4 Look for patterns

Now I need to caveat this exercise.

Sadly, some job ads are poor. The worst bear no relation to the role at hand. You may think I am kidding. I'm not. A few years ago, I applied for a position with a startup that called for 'Knowledge of HCI techniques such as task analysis and state modelling'. I was perplexed, as I expected a startup's focus to be on collaborative product design and testing. At my subsequent interview, I asked how they used these HCI techniques.

"We don't", came the reply.

They asked me why I asked. So, I explained that the information was in the job ad.

It quickly transpired that nobody on the interview panel had reviewed the job ad used to source applicants.

I didn't get the job, and a year later, they used the same job ad again. So, it was probably a blessing.

Let's assume we're working with a good ad and try the same exercise for a sample user researcher role.

Responsibilities

- Work closely with product teams to identify research initiatives
- Design hypotheses and lead studies that examine both user behaviour and attitudes
- Generate actionable insights that both fuel ideation and evaluate product experiences
- Conduct research using a wide variety of qualitative methods and a subset of quantitative methods, such as surveys
- Work cross-functionally with design, product management, content strategy, engineering and marketing
- Communicate results and illustrate suggestions in compelling and creative ways

Minimum Qualifications

- MS/PhD, human behaviour related field (HCI, Psychology, Social Science, Information Science, etc.) 3+ years experience in applied product research
- Command of a broad set of qualitative and user-centred design methods
- Basic understanding of quantitative, behavioural analysis and statistical concepts
- Ability to ask, as well as answer product and user experience related questions
- Compelling communication

Figure 3.5 The important stuff again highlighted

Responsibilities	Minimum qualifications
• Work closely with product teams to identify research initiatives	• MS/PhD, human behaviour related field
• Design hypotheses and lead studies	• 3+ years experience in applied product research
• Generate actionable insights	• Qualitative and user-centred design methods
• Qualitative methods	
• Quantitative methods, such as surveys	• Quantitative, behavioural analysis and statistical concepts
• Work cross-functionally	• Ask/answer product and user experience related questions
• Communicate results	• Compelling communication

Figure 3.6 Just the important stuff for the User Researcher

The user researcher advert also mentions working closely with others, alongside leading studies, and working cross-functionally. They're not looking for somebody to work mainly alone.

So, the user researcher applicant portfolio should also emphasise collaboration in their portfolio.

Also, watch out for specifics - the job ad specifically mentions surveys, so a portfolio with evidence of conducting surveys is likely to fare better than one without.

Taking job ad analysis even further

You can do this exercise individually with a sample of your favoured companies and throw the results into a spreadsheet.

Then you can see what your chosen companies have in common and tailor your portfolio to talk to these shared requirements.

Company A

- Working closely with others
- BA or BFA in related field
- Wireframes and user flows
- Proficient in visual design
- Synthesise feedback from various sources
- IA and IXD skills
- Great communication skills
- Voice of the user

Company C

- Working in cross-functional teams
- BA/BFA or MFA in design, or equivalent experience
- User journeys, prototypes and wireframes
- Visual design sensibilities
- Transform user insights into innovative concepts that solve user needs
- Knowledge of user-centred design principles, IA, UX, and content strategy
- Excellent communication
- Represent the voice of the customer

Company B

- Work closely and collaborate in teams
- BA/BS in related field
- Wireframe, prototype
- Final pixel-perfect mockups
- Turn conceptual ideas into something useful
- UX and IXD experience
- Solid communication skills
- Design advocate

Company D

- Designing in cross-functional teams
- Bachelor's Degree or equivalent in Design
- Storyboards, mockups, and prototypes
- Strong visual design skills
- Distill complicated problems into simple solutions
- Demonstrated experience in crafting usable digital interfaces
- Excellent oral and written communication
- Establish and evangelise the design strategy

Figure 3.7 Key requirements for 4 companies. See where they agree?

Also, have you identified some gaps? Are the companies requesting skills you don't currently have? How can you obtain them? A course? Voluntary activities? Mentoring?

Don't let these gaps put you off applying for a role, particularly if you're female. Most women (and some men that don't match gender norms) won't apply for a job if they don't match the requirements 100%. This is a mistake. Sometimes it's OK to break the rules.

For clarity: Do apply if you don't meet a job's requirements 100% but don't pretend you have any skills or experience you lack. Be in it for the long haul - find ways of getting missing skills. Genuinely have the 'growth mindset' that employers often value.

Support ad analysis with online detective work

Given the variable quality of job ads, it's worth validating them with additional research. Let's take a look at the options.

First, check company websites and social media. What clues do they give away as to how they work and what they value?

Check any employee biographies. Pay attention to their experience, and any company structure implied. Try to work out who you might be working with and how.

Is there a company blog or media section? These may contain industry insights, product announcements, and information about working practices.

Set up a Google Alert[11] to receive an email when the search engine indexes new pages related to your target employer.

---

[11] https://www.google.com/alerts

Use Google news[12] to keep up with company or industry news.

You read job ads for roles you're interested in. Now review the ads for any positions you may work alongside.

Entering an employer's website into the Wayback Machine[13] may allow you to see the ads of jobs that have already been filled and removed from an employer's current website.

Understanding the other available roles may give you insight into the company's organisation and how research and design fit into it.

Are the companies listed on company review websites such as Glassdoor?[14] Does the content look proactively managed? Are there any industry news and blogs online? If so, how is the company perceived externally?

Pay special attention to LinkedIn.[15] Who is working at your chosen companies today? What was their background? Where did they work before? Do the companies favour people with particular experience? The more you can understand company needs, the better.

A simple search of LinkedIn for a company name will reveal if any of your contacts previously worked there or are connected to people who do.

These folks may be able to offer valuable insight and be willing to make an introduction.

---

[12] https://news.google.com/

[13] https://archive.org/web/

[14] https://www.glassdoor.com/

[15] https://www.linkedin.com/

Who do you know who has worked at your chosen companies? Who do you know who knows somebody who has worked there? LinkedIn will tell you. Once you know, be bold - request a coffee or an introduction.

Thinking of making a speculative enquiry? Following your target company on LinkedIn may help you keep up with its current activity.

Want to learn more about your likely hiring manager? Do a LinkedIn search for the company and the manager's most likely job title.

Once you have identified them, check their profile and the groups and interests they follow.

Both of these may help build a picture of what's important to them.

Search SpeakerDeck[16] and SlideShare[17] for past presentations from a company. Any hint of working practices?

Is the company on Twitter, Facebook or other social media? What are they talking about and sharing?

If customers are interacting with them, what are they saying?

---

[16] https://speakerdeck.com/

[17] https://www.slideshare.net/

But also go offline

Do any UX events with networking opportunities take place near you? How about local gatherings by the IxDA,[18] UXPA,[19] SIGCHI,[20] and others?

Here's a neat trick. Use Google to search Meetup[21] or Eventbrite[22] for local events your chosen companies may attend. For example, try searching for site:meetup.com <company name>

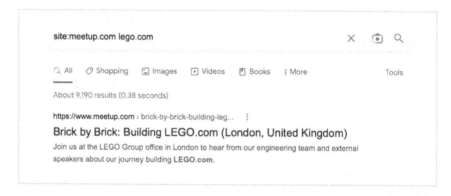

Figure 3.8 This looks like a great event to meet people from LEGO.

Do some prep before you go. Who is going? Is there anyone that you need to seek out? What are you going to ask them?

They're more common in the USA and Asia than in Europe, but look for career fairs where employers invite potential candidates to

[18] https://www.ixda.org/

[19] https://uxpa.org/

[20] https://sigchi.org/

[21] https://www.meetup.com/home/

[22] https://www.eventbrite.com/

visit and learn more about work opportunities. Again, be prepared. Have copies of your résumé or CV printed to share and sensible questions to ask. It's an opportunity to make a great first impression. Use it wisely.

Through your networking efforts, you may find yourself having coffee with somebody from your target employer. This is more than just a valuable opportunity to get the inside track. You could get an internal referral that turns a robust application into an absolute certainty. Referrals by existing employees often bypass human resources checks and go straight to the top of the pile.

As with the networking that leads to it, prepare good, well-researched questions. Don't just sit there in awkward silence. Save that for romantic dates.

Understanding hiring managers

Having discussed ways that you can learn about your users, let me now share some of what I've learned over the past decade.

If you worked as a doctor, another doctor would likely review your application. If you were a lawyer, another lawyer would take the reins. But in the user experience field, the situation is often more complex. The hiring manager could be almost anyone. They could be a fellow UX designer, a project manager, a creative director, a lead developer, a product owner, a marketing professional, or even a small business owner.

These potential employers or clients will all have a different idea of what UX is and what a UX design or research role should involve. At best, they'll have developed a person specification which details what their ideal employee should achieve. At worst, they may only know that they have a problem to solve and that a UX designer may be able to help them.

Also, remember that the hiring manager may not be the actual decision-maker. They may only have permission to put selected portfolios before a more senior manager or a review committee.

What they are looking for will be subjective, influenced by their role, experience, company culture, and other factors.

Let's discuss these now, looking again at corporates, startups, and agencies.

Corporates

As we discussed earlier, it can take a long time for things to be done in many corporates. So, hiring managers often look for perseverance and experience on long projects. The ability to deal skilfully with internal politics is also valued.

Startups

Startups, on the other hand, favour collaboration and speed of delivery. Design leadership consultant Kim Goodwin reckons startups value process skills for bringing order to chaos, but only if it is not called a 'process.'

Agencies

Digital agencies or consultancies will often be interested in seeing a broad portfolio of work and strong examples of attractive documentation. In terms of methodology, waterfall is still common as they're typically paid to produce something and then hand it off to their client. They'll also want evidence of pitch work and strong stakeholder management skills.

The hiring manager's role influences their needs

One of the first presentations on portfolio design was in 2012 by Lynn Teo, then Chief Experience Officer at McCann Erickson.

In the talk, she suggested that a portfolio reviewer's job role profoundly affects what they look for in a portfolio. My research has also confirmed this.

UX leads, Lynn said, will be interested in UX methods, whether the candidate is a team player, and the quality of the work shown.

Project managers will be interested in the overall design process, the candidate's communication skills and whether their work was delivered on time and within budget.

"Creative directors", Lynn continues, "will be interested in conceptual thought, problem statements and the effectiveness of the solutions detailed in the portfolio".

UX maturity may also factor

What a hiring manager is looking for will also be affected by the company's so-called UX maturity… the extent to which UX design has been adopted within the organisation.

Last time I counted, there were about 30 UX maturity models in existence, but they all reflect roughly the same stages of adoption:

- Stage 0: Unrecognised. UX is not important.
- Stage 1: Interested. UX is important but receives little funding.
- Stage 2: Invested. UX is very important, and formalised programs emerge.
- Stage 3: Committed. UX is critical, and executives are actively involved.
- Stage 4: Engaged. UX is one of the core tenets of the organisation.
- Stage 5: UX is in the organisation's fabric; it's not discussed separately.

Hiring managers at less mature organisations will want to see experience in similar organisations. They may be concerned that a designer with most of their experience in UX-mature companies may be frustrated in an environment where UX design is considered something that gets in the way of what stakeholders wish to do.

At less UX-mature organisations, UX designers spend more time on internal education than designing. They may expect to see more of this advocacy or stakeholder management work in your portfolio.

Team size

As a general rule of thumb, small teams need generalists. Big teams can use and may like to see specialists.

Understanding recruiters

Along with hiring managers and peers, your portfolio may also be reviewed by an in-house or external recruiter.

The best recruiters will, with care and attention, match the right person to the right vacancy and facilitate the hiring process until the appointment has been made.

The best recruiters will:

- work with employers on their vacancy specification so that it clearly articulates the experience and skills required
- act as an advocate for a great candidate that wouldn't be considered based solely on their résumé or CV
- provide insight on their client, the current job market, and future trends
- give constructive feedback on a candidate's résumé or CV
- coach a candidate through all aspects of the interview and hiring process

• advise candidates on their careers and what to focus on

External recruiters may also have roles on offer that cannot be found any other way. They may be proactive in finding suitable work for a candidate, suggesting matches as and when they come up. So, ignore the bad PR that recruiters get - a good one is worth knowing.

What a recruiter knows about UX will vary

Some of the larger I.T. recruitment agencies admit to knowing little about UX. They confess to playing a numbers game, submitting as many résumés or CVs as possible to a client in the hope that one or more of their candidates will be called for an interview.

Staff at a specialist UX recruitment agency should know more. They may even have completed a short UX design course and be aware of some basic UX fundamentals. Even so, their knowledge may be skewed by the needs of their existing client base. If, for example, they have dealt mainly with corporate clients, their understanding of UX design will reflect that.

Recruiters will quiz potential candidates based on their client's brief. Some briefs are better than others. In some cases, it may just be a job title.

Ultimately, the route to success with a recruiter is to build a great relationship.

The role of your UX portfolio in this is two-fold: to support your conversations with them and to help the recruiter act as your advocate during any application process.

4. DESIGNING FOR BUSY PEOPLE

If there's one thing that hiring managers and recruiters have in common, it's lack of time.

Hiring managers are typically reviewing portfolios in the few minutes between meetings. They're often in a hurry, needing to draw up a list of potential candidates for an immediate vacancy. They only have a little time.

Recruiters have a similar challenge. Every moment they spend reviewing a portfolio is time they could use talking to a candidate or client. Their job is to connect people. And often, that's what they enjoy doing.

In 2012 the job site TheLadders revealed that recruiters spend about 6 seconds reviewing a CV or résumé before they make the initial 'fit/no fit' decision. (fn)

When it comes to portfolios, the situation is a little better. My research suggests you have 30 seconds or less to make a good impression.

There is one significant difference between recruiters and hiring managers:

• External recruiters are interested in fielding as many candidates as possible. They will review portfolios to rule candidates in.

• Hiring managers want the shortest shortlist they feel comfortable with. They will be looking to rule people out.

In both cases, success is more likely if you design your portfolio for busy people.

Attractive products are perceived as more usable

How your portfolio looks is important.

In my research, I asked hiring managers to show me a portfolio that greatly impressed them. Each time, the portfolio was beautiful, not just well-written.

As Donald Norman wrote, "Aesthetics matter: attractive things work better. Good design means that beauty and usability are in balance." Hiring managers, it seems, succumb as much as anyone to the aesthetic usability effect.

If you do not have graphic design skills, you may feel a little sad at this point. Fear not — the most beautiful UX portfolio didn't always result in a successful hire following the interview.

But the visual appearance of your portfolio — layout, typography, colour — must support your overall message. Otherwise, it will detract from it.

Shorter portfolios generally work better

There's a UX portfolio online that so-called experts recommend as best in class. I removed the client's name from one of its case studies and put it in front of hiring managers. It didn't do well.

The critical problem was its length: 6,200 words. This would take a hiring manager around 25 minutes to read.

And that's just a single case study, not the whole portfolio. No hiring manager has the time to review a portfolio of that length, let alone a single case study.

So, keep your portfolio short. As a rule of thumb, a PDF-based portfolio shouldn't run more than 15 pages, even if you're experienced.

With an online portfolio, lead with your most relevant work.

De-prioritise lower-value case studies, either visually or by placing them within an archive section.

Design your portfolio for the fast and slow track

Remember: the purpose of your UX portfolio is to get you an interview. Hiring managers don't need your life story or a detailed account of your research or design process.

Your portfolio needs to demonstrate your ability to synthesise, prioritise, and communicate essential information about you.

Your portfolio needs to work on two tracks:

• The fast track, where the critical information about you and your work is immediately apparent.

• And the slow track, where the critical information about you and your work is explained and fleshed out.

Graphic design tips

In this section, I will introduce fundamental graphic design principles and tips to help you deliver an attractive portfolio that provides reviewers with both fast and slow tracks. It's not intended to be an in-depth summary of graphic design techniques, but I hope it will get you on the right path. No pun intended.

Use a grid

Whether your portfolio is online or PDF, align typography, images, and graphics to a grid. It'll bring consistency and visual harmony to your page layout. Your portfolio will look neat, clean, and composed. Reviewers will find it easier to navigate through your content.

Maintaining your portfolio will also be easier as you have made many layout designs while choosing your original grid structure, and you won't need to make these decisions again.

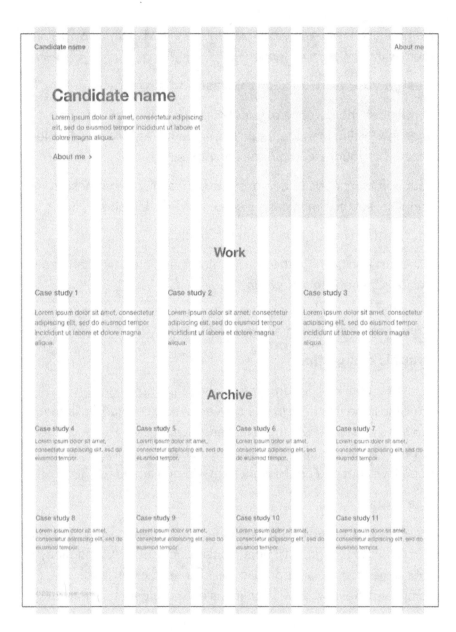

Figure 4.1 A suitable grid for a UX Portfolio website

A simple landscape grid works best for a PDF-based portfolio that could be printed or read on-screen. For the web, designers often opt for a grid with 12 or 24 columns, as 12 and 24 are divisible by 2 and 3. This offers the most flexibility regarding how many elements can be positioned in a row.

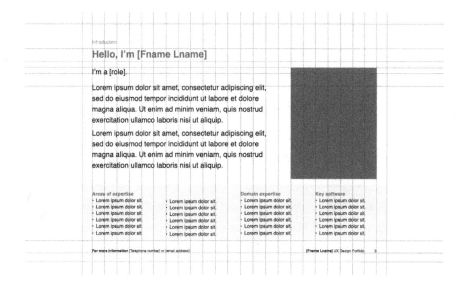

Figure 4.2 A suitable grid for a PDF UX Portfolio

For PDF portfolios, include 'folios and footlines'

If creating a PDF-based portfolio, don't forget to have room in your grid for 'folios and footlines.'

In print publishing, folios are page numbers. Number the pages so you can refer to specific items easily during a screening call or interview.

In an online portfolio, ensure your contact details are always visible

If you have an online portfolio, add your name and contact details to the footer of each page.

Use white space

When you lay out your portfolio, don't pack everything in. It makes your portfolio more difficult to use. It creates the wrong impression. Use white space. Allow your text and images to breathe.

Think about typography

Typography is a crucial way to reflect your personality in your portfolio. Still, it should also be invisible — reviewers should never become aware of the act of reading, or they may stop.

Your choice of typeface is more critical in headlines, but the body copy also has a feel. With both, keep it professional. Choose for your portfolio reviewers, not yourself.

Unless you have visual design expertise, stick to two typefaces at the most. Contrasting fonts will provide the maximum effect—for example, Gill Sans and American Typewriter.

Whichever typefaces you choose, make sure they are legible.

Safe bets include:

> Baskerville, Bembo, Bodoni, Caslon, Clarendon, Frutiger, Futura, Garamond, Gill Sans, Goudy, Helvetica, Janson, Minion, Palatino, Perpetua, Times New Roman, and Univers.

Classic combinations include:

• Helvetica Neue / Garamond

• Futura (Bold) / Bodoni 72

• Garamond (Bold) / Futura

• Georgia / Verdana

Think about text sizing. The smaller that text is, the less critical your reviewer will assume it to be. The larger, the more significant they will consider it. A type size of 12 points is the minimum for both online and print use.

Use ALL CAPS sparingly, if at all - people are more comfortable with reading mixed case.

Use italics sparingly, and underline only for links.

If more than 20% of your portfolio is bold and italic, look at it again. That's way too much.

Use capital letters to start sentences and list items. And for proper nouns such as cities, people, software, and company names. Using them for anything else in the body text (such as roles, techniques, or deliverables) will make your writing choppy and harder to read.

For headings, sentence case and title case are both excellent choices.

Whichever you use, make sure you stick to it.

Set a line-height

The golden ratio is considered aesthetically pleasing, occurring throughout history in geometry, art, and architecture. Some designers believe multiplying type size by the golden ratio (1.618) will result in a good line height. It's a place to start.

Keep line length to ten words a line

Regarding line length for the body copy, aim for around 60 characters. That's about ten words a line.

If you read to the end of a line and find yourself rereading the same line instead of the next one, the line length is too long.

Left-align your text

Left-align your text, including headings. It's the most common arrangement and, therefore, familiar and comfortable to read. It gives a nice, clean left-hand edge for a reviewer's eye to return to.

Avoid right-aligned text. It'll cause a reviewer's eyes to do acrobatics every time they reach the end of a line and try to pick up the next one.

Fully justified text is pretty much the same. Irregular spacing within paragraphs can make the text less easy to read.

Keep centred text to a minimum. Avoid using it for significant amounts of text you really want someone to read.

Place your headings carefully

In multi-column layouts, avoid placing a heading at the top of anything but the first column, as it could draw a reviewer's attention away from the left-hand column altogether.

Stay away from decorative bullets

Avoid the temptation to use a variety of decorative bullets to express your individuality. Gimmicks such as icons or a colour difference will bring confusion rather than support the delivery of your message.

So, please keep it simple. Just one style of bullet throughout.

Never centre the items in a bulleted list, as this camouflages the bulleted list. Always left-align.

Pull-out quotes from users or stakeholders provide a great way of highlighting specific details.

Make them more prominent, but think carefully before putting them in different colours. Colourful text throughout a document will distract.

Always attribute quotes. Several General Assembly graduate portfolios I've reviewed have contained pull-out quotes such as "It's now so much easier to use." When I asked the candidate who said this, they sheepishly admitted that they made the quote up. Don't do this.

Also, I'd be a wealthy person now if I had a pound or a dollar for every Steve Jobs quote I'd seen in a portfolio.

A UX portfolio is about you and what you can do. Inspirational quotes don't tell a reviewer very much. So, leave them out.

Colour can bring your portfolio to life, but as with typography, less is more.

Be a little conservative — choose colours that reflect you and will be appropriate to your prospective employer or client.

Coolors[23] is a great website that generates a colour palette every time you hit the space bar.

If you see a colour you like, you can lock it in and continue to generate suitable partners until you have a full palette you like.

Alternatively, take a look at Color Hunt.[24] It offers a seemingly never-ending list of colour palettes for your consideration.

---

[23] https://coolors.co/

[24] https://colorhunt.co/

Finally on colour, the website Adobe Color[25] offers several tools, but Extract Theme[26] derives a colour palate from an image you upload.

Handling images and photographs

I mentioned that portfolios must support both the fast and the slow track. Photographs are perfect for the fast track — you can use them to draw attention to particular aspects of a case study or story.

So, don't just throw images into your portfolio without care. Use photographs and carefully-worded captions to communicate your key messages.

Check that each photo conveys the message it is intended to.

The vast majority of the photographs in your portfolio should reinforce your written narrative.

Ensure the content of the photograph is visible. The image should be cropped to draw attention to the correct elements. It should be of the highest quality, not out of focus or pixelated.

Where you include a cut-out of a deliverable, ensure users can tell the work is tidy, even if you can't show the detail.

Ensure your image are sized appropriately.

For an online portfolio, avoid thumbnail images that require the reviewer to click or tap to see anything of value.

Remember that hiring managers have little time, and the less work they have to do, the better.

---

25 https://color.adobe.com/

26 https://color.adobe.com/create/image

Ensure photographs look professional but not overly so. The images need to look credible and realistic, but not like stock photography. Oh, and never use stock photography in your portfolio. It's your portfolio, not Getty's!

Avoid framing or embedding photographs and images into browser chrome or a device like an iPhone.

It'll only result in a picture that will quickly date.

Should you include photographs of yourself in your portfolio?

Some people think that doing so can introduce the opportunity for sexism, racism, ageism and other issues.

Others say go ahead — you wouldn't want to work for a company with those values. It's a personal decision.

If you decide to include a photograph of yourself, appear professional and approachable. It would be best if you conveyed that you are someone the portfolio reviewer would want to work with. Save the Halloween photo for another time.

Look the part. Dress appropriately. Adopt the same rule for face-to-face interviews — dress for the job you want, not the one you have. Corporate or smart casual? Choose well.

Make sure that you sleep well the night before. Before the photo is taken, get a haircut. Look your best. Do something for yourself. Do what you can to arrive feeling good about yourself.

Think about how to handle any piercings, tattoos, and jewellery you have. Will they lead to a good or bad first impression for your ideal client or employer? Should you hide them or focus attention on them? Again, choose well.

Think carefully about where to have the photo taken. Ensure you are front and centre, not lost to a distracting background.

Use captions

Captions are fantastic. Use them to add detail to the message a photograph is communicating. Place them under the picture. That's where people expect them. Left-justify the caption and have it extend no more than three-quarters of the image's width, even if the caption extends to two lines. Doing this lets in a little white space that will allow the page or screen to breathe a little.

Use infographics wisely

Use charts and graphs to illustrate exciting data.

Follow best information design practice. Use charts and graphs to show cause and effect or to make visual comparisons. Demonstrate the impact of your design work against an important metric over time.

Remember, the goal of information design is for people to understand as much as possible in the shortest possible time. Keep the ratio of data to decorative elements high.

If a table or list would be more effective, use a table or list. Don't hesitate to lose the pretty graph.

Don't be tempted to display your skills in the form of a bar chart.

Figure 4.3 A useless skill bar

After all, what does 80% or 3 out of 5 stars mean in terms of Figma or Sketch skill?

It means nothing. And you'll have just told the portfolio reviewer you know nothing about good information design.

Also, be wary of presenting your career as a timeline.

Careers can be messy things, and timelines can quickly become congested.

It's often more effective to use a simple table or list.

Documents and artefacts are essential. They help us work through and develop ideas. Documents also help us persuade, inform and involve other people.

But they're part of our job, not all of it. We shouldn't encourage hiring managers to judge us on our documents alone.

As a general rule, avoid providing complete documents and artefacts. Use them in the same way as photographs instead.

Deliver enough of the document to communicate your point and no more. Crop so only the essential is shown. Then add a caption.

Handling documents and artefacts this way allows you to put them fully into context.

Video requires more interest and engagement from people than words and pictures on a page.

For this reason, use it sparingly and with good reason. Edit it tightly for length, too — factor in the portfolio reviewer's lack of time. Provide a transcript.

And if using a clip from a usability research session, ensure you respect privacy laws and show that you have. Hiring managers will notice if you don't.

Write effectively

In this final section, let's talk about writing.

If a hiring manager isn't reviewing your portfolio alone in-between meetings, they're probably doing so on their solo commute home.

So, write to an individual, not a group.

Be informal, but not too much. Use contractions and break the occasional rule — start some sentences with 'But' or 'And.'

Avoid overselling

Drop the hyperbole if you want to be taken seriously.

If in doubt, write as you speak. I've critiqued hundreds of portfolios over the past few years. When I can't understand a sentence, I ask the portfolio owner to explain the text further. What they reply with is always much clearer than what they've written.

Use active voice

Writing in an active voice rather than a passive voice will bring your stories alive.

In passive voice, the subject of the sentence is acted upon. For example:

> Collaborative workshops were attended by key stakeholders.

In active voice, the subject of the sentence is performing the action. It's much stronger:

> Key stakeholders attended collaborative workshops.

Think short

As advertising legend David Ogilvy famously wrote, "Use short words, short sentences, and short paragraphs."

Aim for 20 words or less per sentence and five sentences per paragraph.

However, don't take David Ogilvy's advice on writing literally.

It's boring if every sentence is the same length.

Vary the sentences to avoid monotony and boredom.

Look to create a pleasant rhythm, not this.

In general, stick to one point or message per sentence.

That's a good rule of thumb.

More complex text will slow portfolio reviewers down.

Watch for commas

If there's more than one, you can probably simplify the sentence. Or maybe it's time to use a list.

Avoid jargon

As the novelist and journalist George Orwell advised, 'Never use a foreign phrase, a scientific word or a Jargon word if you can think of an everyday English equivalent.'

Jargon tends to obscure meaning, so lose it.

Even the most experienced UX practitioners will be grateful.

Essential words only

When editing (not writing), ensure that every word is essential.

Each word should earn its place on the page.

If it is possible to lose a word, don't hesitate to remove it.

Use lists

If you can use bullets to list content, then do so.

A single sentence followed by a list of two items is easier to read than a sentence full of commas.

Try to avoid two or more levels of bullets. Re-write your content instead.

Link purposefully

Sending a portfolio reviewer off to another website or prototype involves risk. Link out only when you believe there is real value in doing so.

Make sure you regularly check any links you include. Don't just verify that the website exists. Ensure the content is also what you expect.

There's no value in sending hiring managers to a website that has changed significantly since you worked on it.

If you want to include links in your PDF portfolio, use a link shortener and give the short URL as the link.

It means reviewers can still view the URL if they print the PDF portfolio.

You can also track how many times the link has been used.

5. PLANNING YOUR UX PORTFOLIO

I'm sure you might be tempted to begin thinking about what to share in your portfolio, but jumping straight to implementation will likely result in a UX Portfolio that misses the mark. Planning your portfolio is critical.

So, we'll look at that in this chapter, covering platform, structure, and curation.

Portfolio platforms

Let's talk about the platform - the form in which you're going to deliver your portfolio.

One question that seems to torment many people is whether their portfolio should be a PDF, a personal website or within a portfolio community like Behance or Dribbble.

There are pros and cons to each platform. Let's take a look.

PDF-based portfolios

My research suggests that many hiring managers prefer PDF-based portfolios.

They're simple to navigate.

They're also easy to share internally.

They're easily printed, and reviewers can scribble notes on top. These notes may then guide a subsequent interview.

For a candidate, a vital benefit of the PDF portfolio is that you can customise them for specific job applications.

If you use a presentation app such as Keynote, PowerPoint or Google Slides, you can hide any case studies you don't wish to include and then export your portfolio to PDF.

But why stop there? You can also customise the portfolio cover and even the introduction.

The more relevant the portfolio, the more likely you will get an interview.

Creating a PDF portfolio is also relatively easy. Apple Keynote, PowerPoint or Google Slides is all you need.

Plus, PDF portfolios are less reliant on the Internet. If sent as an attachment, there's less risk of people being unable to view if a website or the internet is down.

Another pro — No hosting fees.

Cons? The problem with PDF portfolios is that they lack, somewhat ironically given their name, portability - they work well viewed via a PC, Mac or tablet, but on a smartphone? Not so much.

And while it's technically possible to add video and audio to a PDF document, many tools that export to PDF do not support this.

If you do decide to opt for a PDF portfolio, I've got seven tips for you to consider:

1. Do export to actual PDF rather than use a file format that hiring managers may need help to open. I once received a portfolio in Open Office format. It took me 30 minutes to download the necessary tools to export and see it. Had the candidate not been a personal contact, I wouldn't have bothered. I ended up converting the portfolio to PDF for my boss!

2. Don't switch page orientation mid-PDF. From portrait to landscape or landscape to portrait — it isn't enjoyable for anyone reviewing it on-screen.

3. Avoid exporting your entire portfolio as a single-page PDF. This can be unwieldy to navigate on-screen and makes the document impractical to print. Have multiple pages, and make sure you number each one. Start each new case study or significant content item on a new page.

4. Watch the file size. Keep your PDF portfolio less than 10 megabytes to increase the chances of email systems accepting it as an attachment. 5 megabytes is even better. If the program you're using to create your portfolio creates overly-large PDFs, consider using a compression app like PDF squeezer[27] on the Mac to reduce the file size.

5. If you want to make your PDF portfolio available via a file storage site instead, host it at more than one — employer firewalls often block them. For example, they might block Google Drive, not Dropbox[28], or vice versa. Alternatively, host the file on your own website.

6. Include your name in the filename so reviewers can quickly identify your portfolio once they save it to their hard drive. "UX-Portfolio.pdf" won't stand out. You may wish to include the date you created the portfolio too.

7. Avoid adding password protection to the PDF. It'll just act as a barrier. You'll force the viewer to have to find the accompanying email with the password in. They could be looking through your portfolio instead of doing that. So, don't do it.

---

[27] https://www.witt-software.com/pdfsqueezer/

[28] https://www.dropbox.com/

Web-based portfolios

A web-based portfolio has some advantages going for it:

- It can be indexed by search engines and can act as ongoing public promotion every day and night.
- An easy-to-remember web address is easy to share.
- Responsive web design techniques can increase the chance that people can view your portfolio regardless of the device they use.

However:

- Printing is more difficult.
- Internet access is required at the time of the portfolio review.
- Reviewers will judge you on the experience your website offers. So, choosing a suitable template or building your own really well is essential.
- Greater learning curve. Building your own website from scratch will take time that may be better spent working on content.
- It's hard to tailor for different job applications.
- Hosting costs money.

I have some more tips if you decide to opt for a web portfolio.

1. Exercise best web design practice. Ensure the website is responsive. Ensure the interaction design and information architecture are as efficient for visitors as possible. Keep both code weight and the required human interaction low. Don't make reviewers jump through hoops to get what they need. They won't.

2. Don't create placeholder pages that deliver the message "Coming soon!" when viewed. It's an anti-climax for people and a waste of their time. Only create pages when the content is also ready to go live.

3. Regularly check all of the website links you reference. No hiring manager wants to be met with '404 page not found.' If you move your portfolio to a new web address, always arrange for the original URL to redirect visitors to the new one.

4. What do you want a hiring manager to do after they click on your portfolio link? Review your portfolio or hunt for a password? As with PDF portfolios, avoid the obstacle of password protection if you can.

Having spoken about the front end of the website, let's talk about the backend. Does it matter if you use a site builder or a template theme?

It shouldn't do unless the job role you are applying for includes front-end development. If it does, you should probably roll your own.

Whether you choose Squarespace[29], WordPress.com[30], or a personal installation of WordPress[31] with a purchased theme, the important thing is that you find a professional-looking solution that allows you to communicate your story the way you wish to tell it.

Squarespace is a popular choice with many designers. It's template-based, but you can make enough changes to make the template your own.

---

[29] https://www.squarespace.com/

[30] https://wordpress.com/

[31] https://wordpress.org/

If your budget is low, then Medium[32] is an option others have used.[33]

Portfolio communities

Portfolio communities like Behance[34] or Dribbble[35] aren't the best choice for a UX portfolio. They're often image-led. They favour eye candy and don't tend to suit the text-led needs of the UX designer or researcher.

Another issue with portfolio communities is that your competitors are often just one click away.

A recruiter once told me he'd been sent a link to a portfolio on Dribbble.

He was impressed by it, only to realise that he'd taken a wrong turn and was viewing another designer's work instead. This was good for the recruiter, who now had another prospective candidate to contact. It wasn't so good for the original applicant.

Portfolio communities can also be problematic when the portfolio has to be shared internally within a company.

As Erik Flowers of Intuit wrote in a 2013 blog post:[36]

> 'I have to send your materials to upper management. They have never heard of these niche sites. I've had to give

---

32 https://medium.com/

33 https://medium.com/borahm-cho

34 https://www.behance.net/

35 https://dribbble.com/

36 https://erik-flowers.medium.com/what-ive-learned-as-a-ux-interviewer-38fa3e2ec0ab

people's Behance (or whatever) to Sr. Executives who have no idea what they're looking at. "Is this their website? Why are the pictures so small? The URL didn't work. Why is the name different?" Once, when a candidate sent a Dribbble profile, my boss clicked and clicked the thumbnail, and when I told him "those don't enlarge," he looked at me and said, "This is how people want to present their work?"'

So, use a portfolio community only if you're confident that doing so will meet employer needs.

Video portfolios

Occasionally I'm asked if a video portfolio would work. It would undoubtedly have novelty value.

The big problem is that it would also require greater engagement from a reviewer. My research suggests that many won't have the time to sit and watch.

Plus, you're potentially opening yourself up to bias.

In a 2013 study,[37] researchers found that compared to job seekers meeting face to face, job seekers on video were rated as less likeable and less likely to be recommended for a job. While the scenario is different, a video portfolio will likely carry similar baggage.

So, leave video as a component of your portfolio. Please don't make it the whole thing.

---

[37] https://dailynews.mcmaster.ca/articles/two-thumbs-down-for-video-conference-job-interviews/

Other platforms

Believe it or not, I have seen designers use the Google Play store[38] or Apple Books[39] to host their portfolios.

The challenge with both is that they introduce additional steps for a hiring manager that may act as a barrier. They can no longer click on a single link. They have to do that and download an app or ebook.

The most straightforward approach - a website or PDF - is the most effective.

A website or a PDF?

So, we've gone through the options. But people always ask me which one. A website or a PDF?

Ultimately, it depends on who will review your portfolio and what they expect. As I mentioned earlier, many hiring managers prefer the simplicity of a PDF portfolio. But there are still those who believe UX designers should have a web-based portfolio because the role often involves interaction design. So, it's essential to research your prospective portfolio reviewers and anticipate their expectations. I've never heard of a hiring manager rejecting either format outright. They have preferences, not absolutes.

I would start with the PDF first. As I discussed, it's easiest to pull together.

Once that's complete, create a companion website. Rather than deliver the whole portfolio, perhaps offer project summaries and invite visitors to get in touch for further information.

---

[38] https://play.google.com/store/apps

[39] https://www.apple.com/uk/apple-books/

Then when somebody does contact you, customise a PDF UX portfolio just for them. If they're not impressed, they're not worth your interest.

Portfolio format & structure

As you know, most reviewers have limited time to look at portfolios. The more we can do to make things easier for them, the better.

Over the past few years, a standard format for UX portfolios has emerged. The closer you adhere to this skeleton, the quicker a reviewer can focus on understanding your content.

PDF-based portfolios

PDF portfolios typically open with a cover.

Then content about the portfolio owner.

The bulk of the portfolio is case studies.

This is followed by complementary information such as:

• the training courses the portfolio owner has completed

• the events they have spoken at, or perhaps

• client testimonials

Web-based portfolios

Turning to the web portfolio, there's a home page that links off to:

• Case studies

• About me content, and

• A contact page.

For reasons unknown, few web-based portfolios seem to have additional pages of information on training, public speaking, etc. But there's no reason why they can't.

Case study sandwich

In both cases, it's possible to think of the UX portfolio as a case study sandwich.

It leads with introductory content about the portfolio owner. This content must demonstrate immediate connection or value to the prospective employer or client.

Then you have the case studies. These stories provide evidence that you can do what the prospective employer or client needs you to do.

Finally, particularly in the case of the PDF portfolio, there's a closing collection of additional information intended to complete gaps, build credibility, or provide a more rounded image of the portfolio owner.

Portfolio curation

Let's talk about curation - how you select and organise the content of your UX portfolio.

Many hiring managers consider curation an essential design skill. They tell me that many of the portfolios they see are poorly curated, leaving them to choose their own journey through a mass of material. The longest portfolio I have ever seen was a colossal 264 pages.

A few years ago, I met Design Leader Ken Musgrave. At the time, he worked for Dell as Executive Director of Experience Design. Here's what he had to say:

> "I will actually go into Acrobat and I will erase all the crap from a portfolio, and then re-evaluate that portfolio with the more interesting body of work on behalf of other designers that should have done it on their own.

More than once, I've done that and it's like 'Wow!' When you look through that lens, this is a very different candidate than the one that showed every product they've ever worked on.

Sometimes, you'll see designers think they need to show breadth of work or 'I've got a lot of experience,' and just a couple of projects will demonstrate some experience.

We'd far rather have two, three fantastic projects than two or three fantastic projects surrounded by a lot of mediocrity."

Go online, and you'll often see advice that states you must have 3 to 5 case studies.

Beware of anyone who states that you must present things a certain way or in a specific order. There are rules of thumb. But your goal is to create a portfolio that speaks for you, not to create a carbon copy clone that lacks differentiation.

So, Ken's right. Opt for quality over quantity.

Sometimes two case studies are better than five.

So, how do you choose which work to show?

I have a suggestion for you to consider.

Remember this from earlier?

Responsibilities	Minimum qualifications
• Conceptual ideas into something useful and valuable for users	• Communication skills
• Incredibly simple and elegant design flows and experiences	• Strategic product thinking and vision
• Strategic decisions with product and executive team	• Building and shipping applications or software
• Give and solicit feedback from other designers	• Examples of interaction design work
• Partner to oversee the user experience of a product from conception until launch	• End-to-end (hybrid UX and **UI**) product design
	• Execute on visual and interaction details

Figure 5.1 The Product Designer ad revisited

It's the output from when we analysed a product designer job ad.

Let's take the responsibilities and jot down against each one the client/project name and the matching evidence we have.

Here are a couple of things to consider when you do this:

• Exercise some restraint if you have several projects or activities that could sit against a single need. Nobody wants to hear the same story several times. So, write down the project or activity you think is the best. For example, it might be similar work in the same business sector or on the same type of project.

• Don't list mediocre work. List your best work. Put down only what you want to do - the kind of work you want to be doing.

Responsibilities	Evidence
• Conceptual ideas into something useful and valuable for users	• Together - sending a message
• Incredibly simple and elegant design flows and experiences	• **Snupps** - onboarding
• Strategic decisions with product and executive team	• **Snupps** - team workshop
• Give and solicit feedback from other designers	• Virgin media - weekly peer review
• Partner to oversee the user experience of a product from conception until launch	• BT - buzz project

Figure 5.3 The Snupps project figures strongly

Once you've completed this exercise, you may have some projects you didn't jot down.

If so, those projects aren't an excellent match for the role. By all means, double-check. But don't force them into your portfolio.

Having added all your evidence, reflect on it for a moment or two. Are there any significant gaps? Perhaps the job isn't that good a match for you today. So, your goal becomes attaining the evidence that you need to take the role in future.

Does a particular project figure strongly? Have you mentioned a project more than once, as in this example?

If so, consider prioritising it for a detailed recap. Summarise the others.

If you've completed this exercise, you now know the case studies you have to write. And without mental anguish!

Isn't that lovely?

6. FIRST IMPRESSIONS

In this chapter, we'll look at making the right first impression, focusing on the first few pieces of content that a portfolio reviewer will see.

My first piece of advice is to lead your portfolio with your name.

Figure 6.1 Portfolio example

This portfolio homepage is aesthetically pleasing. It creates an excellent first impression - but the creator's name isn't mentioned.

The introduction

This is the small block of text that leads your UX Portfolio. It's your first opportunity to connect with a prospective employer or client. You need to start strong and maintain it. It's the first place to start communicating your uniqueness as a designer or researcher. Sadly, many designers and researchers get it wrong.

Tobias van Schneider, who created the portfolio tool Semplice[40], highlighted the issue in a 2015 blog post:[41]

> "While reviewing hundreds of portfolios, one of the most common things I discovered are headlines such as: "I craft meaningful experiences" or "I push perfect pixels." combined with a random stock photo of a Macbook sitting on a desk. These intros not only take up a lot of space but are also used by 90% of other designers and do not contribute anything to your uniqueness as a designer."

In 2013, Alex Corneal created 'the worst portfolio ever'[42] to highlight the worst trends in portfolio design. The sample introduction is typical of that often found online:

> "I am a 23 year old designer/thinker living and making in sunny San Francisco. A penetrating storyteller, I like to massage my hand-crafted, beautiful pixels. I'm obsessed with kitesurfing, minimalism and making things easier and more delightful. I make stuff, I ship stuff, and I like creating engaging visual experiences for real people. I also like craft beers and whales."

---

[40] https://www.semplice.com/

[41] https://vanschneider.com/avoid-these-5-things-when-building-your-design-portfolio

[42] https://web.archive.org/web/20211229083556/http://theworstportfolioever.com/

Sadly, little has changed since the post. Hiring managers and recruiters get used to seeing the same thing. Try a Google search for the phrase "I design products that people love."

Lose the hyperbole

Often, people have fallen into a giant vat of marketing speak. This is not only a problem with portfolios. As UX Manager Kim Bieler wrote in a 2015 blog post[43], it affects resumes and CVs too:

> "I love these resumes because after I get done rolling my eyes, I have fun imagining the candidate squirm when I ask them to: Tell me about a time when you 'broke the boundaries of design. Explain exactly how this solution was visionary. Give me an example of an 'unforgettable' user experience you designed and how you determined that no one has ever forgotten it."

> "I kid! I would never humiliate a fellow UX designer like that. I just wouldn't call them at all."

Kim's advice to avoid arrogant overselling is to ask yourself if you are prepared to defend your extraordinary claims with actual, believable examples. For example, are you truly an out-of-the-box thinker or just someone who'd like to be? How could you demonstrate that?

Keep it short and focused

You don't have to write much. 40 words or 240 characters is more than enough. In other words, just under a tweet.

_____

[43] https://web.archive.org/web/20201101011128/http://www.uxresume.com/confidence-or-arrogance-how-to-tell-when-your-resume-has-crossed-the-line/

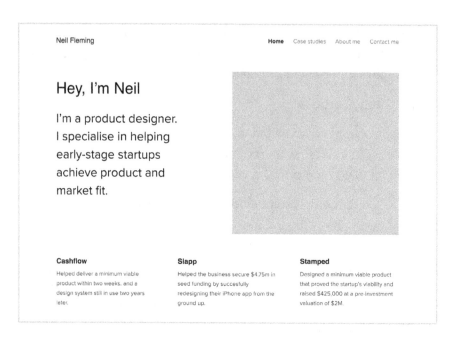

Figure 6.2 Well done, Neil!

Here's where most people start[44]:

> Hey, I'm Neil
>
> UX Designer & Researcher

The job role. In this case, UX designer and researcher. This is factually correct, perhaps, but there's no indication why Neil is the right person for the job against so many other applicants.

> Hey, I'm Neil
>
> UX Designer passionate about research

Oh, he's passionate about research. Shouldn't all designers be passionate about research? This is not enough.

---

[44] Every example the fictitious Neil came up with exists online, describing an actual live designer. Apart from the final one.

> Hey, I'm Neil
>
> I'm a product designer based in Dallas.

Neil added his location. I bet there are other product designers in Dallas. This isn't enough. He tries adding a specialism:

> Hey, I'm Neil
>
> I'm a product designer specialising in prototyping and user interface design.

Wouldn't you expect a product designer to specialise in these things? No, not good enough. At this point, Neil goes a bit nuts:

> Hey, I'm Neil
>
> I'm focusing on moving people through holistic, relevant experiences and bringing artistry to projects I'm a part of.

Would you want to work with Neil?

Many designers struggle because they believe their portfolio introduction is about explaining the kind of designer they are and what interests them. In contrast, portfolio reviewers want to start learning how the designer can meet their needs.

So, try to think about what your portfolio reviewer needs to know. Are they looking for a breadth of experience or specialist knowledge? Are they looking for specific skills? Whatever it is, try to refer to it in your introduction. After a lie-down, Neil tries again with a mini biography:

> Hey, I'm Neil
>
> I'm a staff designer at Lyft. Previously a Lead at Google. I give design workshops and share design tutorials on YouTube.

This is a move in the right direction. But it has one problem - it needs to focus more on the employer or client's needs. The fact that he has worked at Lyft and Google is strong, but the fact that he shares design tutorials on YouTube is unlikely to be relevant unless he's going for a teaching position.

The fictitious Neil can do better.

> Hey, I'm Neil
>
> I'm a product designer. I specialise in helping early-stage startups achieve product and market fit.

Finally, Neil gets it. He's a product designer specialising in helping early-stage startups achieve product and market fit.

I'd read further if I worked for a startup. I'd be hungry to see case studies of how he previously helped other startups achieve what he describes.

Again, avoid the hyperbole and over-selling

If you're starting your career, avoid implying that you're an experienced hand. Selling yourself as an accomplished strategist when you only have course projects in your portfolio will be noticed eventually.

In my experience, overselling like this often occurs in portfolios from UX boot camp participants. Please don't do it.

Explain your circumstances and what you are looking for instead:

> In October, I will graduate with a Master of Science in User Experience Design at Kent State University. I am currently looking for an internship as a product designer.

Personalise if you can

If you're producing a PDF portfolio for a specific client or employer, add their name or the vacancy reference to your portfolio cover. It indicates that you created the portfolio specifically for them, which may help you stand out.

Reflect your personality with an image

If you are considering accompanying your introduction with a photograph, don't overlook the opportunity to use an image that reflects your personality.

Adrienne Hunter's PDF-based portfolio opens with a photo of her holding a banana as if it was a telephone. Fun!

ADRIENNE HUNTER
DESIGN PORTFOLIO

I am an interdisciplinary problem solver and I do it through user experience design.

Demo Feedback
- reception issues
- ergonomics could be improved
- no volume control
- visual display?

Figure 6.3 Adrienne Hunter's Portfolio Cover

Case study titles

If the intro is the first opportunity to show hiring managers how relevant you are, your case study titles are the second.

Unfortunately, hiring managers are often met with this:

Figure 6.4 "Mystery meat navigation"

The owner of this portfolio expects the hiring manager to hover over each image to get each case study title:

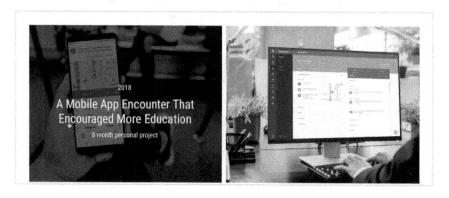

Figure 6.5 Case study title only visible on mouser

No comparison of case study titles is possible. Perhaps reviewers should click at random. They probably will.

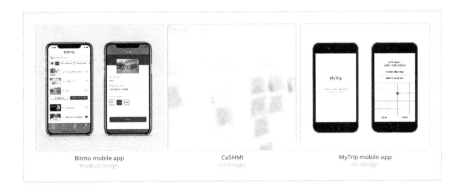

Figure 6.6 Project name and responsibility

Sometimes, portfolio owners give the project name and their responsibility: product design, UX design, and UX research. These labels offer little value.

Using the artefact or what was worked on is just as weak:

Figure 6.7 Artefacts and what was worked on

Some portfolio owners choose to describe what the website or app they worked on does.

Figure 6.8 What it does

"Help educators discover products, programs, and resources that are easy to use and support student success."

It's meaningful but rarely what a hiring manager wants to know. They want to know what the portfolio owner did and achieved.

This is a further step in the right direction:

Figure 6.9 What it achieved for customers

"Designed a first-of-its-kind mileage tracking product to help Lyft driver record all their tax-deductible miles, increasing driver savings by 400 million dollars."

However, like the other introductions, it doesn't directly relate to a hiring manager's need. How about this one?

Figure 6.10 Improvements to be made

"Improving usability, discoverability and conversion for luxury fashion brand Mulberry." That sounds like something a hiring manager might be interested in. Indicating the results achieved would make the portfolio stronger.

Figure 6.11 What was achieved for the business

"Building a design practice and team: How we grew our team at Shopify Toronto."

Matching an evident hiring manager need works well.

If I was looking for a UX manager with experience growing a design team at a household name, I couldn't click or tap fast enough to read this case study.

How about these?

Figure 6.12 What was achieved

"Transforming a global corporate culture. Empowering communities during disaster. Bringing government to the people." This is the portfolio of somebody who knows how to design to connect people on a significant scale. It's a great example of how case study titles can work together to create a strong impression.

Stuck generating titles? Try the X-Y-Z formula

Former Google Chief Human Resources Officer Laszlo Bock developed the X-Y-Z formula for displaying achievements on a resumé.[45] This is it:

> Accomplished [X] as measured by [Y] by doing [Z]

---

[45] https://www.linkedin.com/pulse/20140929001534-24454816-my-personal-formula-for-a-better-resume/

"In other words," Bock says, "start with an active verb, numerically measure what you accomplished, provide a baseline for comparison, and detail what you did to achieve your goal."

For example:

> Amazon Prime Music
>
> Increased the median number of active customers by 186% over ten months by addressing customer pain points related to music browsing and discovery.

Another example:

> Shopify
>
> Growing the design team from 5 to 30 over 18 months by developing design foundations, a common understanding, and the company's first intern programme.

Be as specific as possible. If the project had multiple positive outcomes, use the most impactful.

If stuck on the beneficial result, remember that portfolio reviewers are interested in employing staff who can:

• increase profits

• sell more

• gain market share

• raise quality

• enhance customer satisfaction

• improve efficiency

• reduce costs

What did your project achieve?

How long should a title be?

I'm sure you noticed that the title examples just shared run between 21-28 words. This is no accident. When it comes to headlines, longer is better. Science says so.

In 2015, neuroscience lab Nielsen Neuro and tech company Sharethrough hooked 226 people up to EEG machines for a non-invasive scan of electrical activity in the brain. They were looking at brain activity in response to text. Their study revealed that headlines between 21 and 28 words maximised engagement.[46]

---

[46] https://www.sharethrough.com/blog/the-1-072-words-that-will-change-how-you-write-headlines-forever

About me

If you have an About me page, it ought to build on your introduction.

Like the introduction, it should explain what you can offer your prospective employer or client.

Your goals:

1. Explain in simple terms what you can do for the portfolio reviewer.

2. Build credibility as a prospective employee or consultant.

3. Demonstrate that you are likeable and worth working with.

4. Give reviewers the next step — to examine your case studies or get in touch.

There's a simple template that may help you start. I have been unable to find the original author of it. It runs like this:

> I'm a [what you are]
>
> I help [who you help and what you do]
>
> When I'm not [doing what you do for work]
>
> you can find me [doing what you do outside work]
>
> Want to work together? I'd love to hear from you.

For example:

> I'm a user researcher.
>
> I help start-ups, and companies like IBM and HP learn about their users.
>
> When I'm not helping product teams make intelligent decisions, you can find me on my couch watching Seinfeld.

About me

I'm an experienced design leader with a strong background in designing for large organisations across web and mobile.

I've led and delivered work across the entire project lifecycle using design approaches that are thoughtful, human-centred, strategic, and evidence-based.

I help shape UX practice globally and locally as a board director with the IxDA and as a London local leader through initiatives, events, teaching and mentorship.

Figure 6.13 Boon Yew Chew's About me page

Want to work together? I'd love to hear from you."

A variation, used by experience design manager Boon Yew Chew, runs like this:

I'm [what you are].

I've [what you've done].

I help [who you help and what you do].

Either of these templates should get you off the starting blocks.

Adapt, extend and edit your biography until you have something you are comfortable with.

Professional associations

Membership of specific professional associations such as the IxDA[47] and UXPA[48] suggests that you keep up to date with the design industry and develop valuable contacts.

If you're changing your career to UX design from another field, membership in a professional association can indicate that you are serious about making a career shift.

Just add a line to your About me page.

---

[47] https://www.ixda.org/

[48] https://uxpa.org/

At a glance

'At a glance' summarises key metrics and achievements. Optional, it follows 'About me' in a PDF portfolio or sits underneath the main biography in a web-based portfolio.

Use 'At a glance' to highlight:

• key statistics

• years of experience

• awards

• professional association membership

• any other information that will enhance your credibility.

Hello, I'm Ian Fenn.

I help the world's best companies research, design, and develop practical solutions that meet business and user needs.

At a glance

21 years of experience in UX research and design

200+ projects successfully delivered

Career highlights

 Delivering huge, loyal audiences for the BBC, UKTV, and other broadcasters.

Increasing online sales for The Walt Disney Company, international banks, and global retailers.

 Reducing customer support costs for BT, JustGiving, and others.

Your project here? Call me on +44 (0)7734 101672, or email ian@chopstixmedia.com

 Increasing staff productivity at Schlumberger, BP, and Tenaris.

 Retaining more Virgin Media customers, beating stock market expectations.

Helping a startup, Snupps, secure $5 million (£3 million) of seed capital.

Figure 6.14 At a glance example

Core skills

It's fair to say that there is no consistency in job titles and the skills required to fulfil them. The responsibilities and skill requirements necessary for a UX Designer role at one company may differ at another.

It is helpful to list the skills that you have.

Essential skills to consider listing (if you have them):

• Design leadership
• User research
• Information architecture
• Interaction design
• Content strategy and copywriting
• Information design
• UX writing
• Visual design
• Prototyping
• Usability evaluation

My core skills

I act as an integral part of a project team or as a UX coach, mentoring clients and advising on best research and design practice. I can work tactically or strategically and am happy doing both.

Experience strategy
Vision-setting, making and guiding effective decisions, running collaborative design activities, influencing others and building consensus.

Information architecture
Identification and organisation of site content and functionality. Card sorting, tree testing, and other techniques. Producing sitemaps, application maps and user interface specifications.

Content strategy
The planning, development, and management of content. Activities including content audits, copywriting, and editing.

Information design
Presenting information to facilitate efficient and effective understanding.

Presentation
Pitching and storytelling.

Design research
Helping teams learn about users and their needs. Research plans, usability testing, interviews, site visits, participatory design, and web analytics analysis.

Interaction design
Creating engaging interfaces that meet user and business goals. Creation of prototypes and wireframes.

Podcasting and radio production
Researching, writing, recording and editing for podcasts and radio programmes.

Front-end development
Coding including HTML, CSS, and JavaScript.

UX recruitment and development
Hiring for UX. Coaching and mentoring.

Figure 6.15 Core skills example

Client list

Once you've gained experience, listing the brands or clients you have worked with can boost your credibility, particularly if their logos are well known.

Consider organising them by business sector or project type if you wish to demonstrate a breadth of experience:

- B2B
- Banking
- Broadcasting
- Corporate
- Ecommerce
- FinTech
- Intranet
- Non-profit, government, and regulatory
- Retail
- Social media
- Tech company
- Tech start-up
- Travel

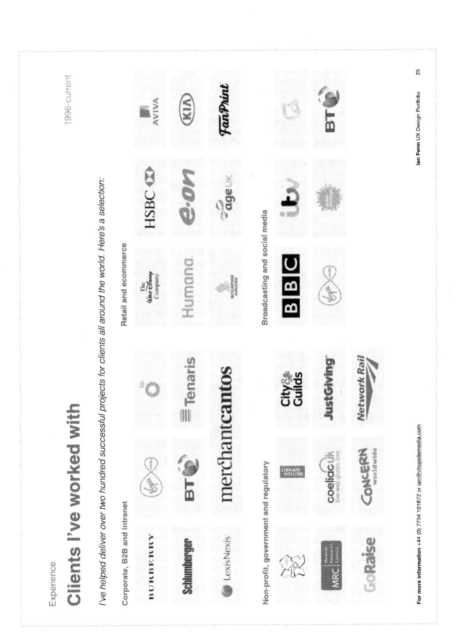

Figure 6.16 Client list example

113

What not to include in your portfolio

I've seen all of the following items in UX portfolios. I wish I hadn't. Hiring managers may not react positively to them.

Whether you're left-brained, right-brained, or both

You may be familiar with the concept of left-brained and right-brained people. It's claimed that individuals who use the right side of their brains most are more creative, spontaneous and subjective. Those who predominantly use the left side of their brain are more logical, detail-oriented and analytical.

Sadly, no evidence supports this idea, and a researcher or designer should know that.

Your Myers-Briggs Type Indicator

As popular as it is during team-building away days, there's just no evidence behind it. Yes, a researcher or designer ought to know this too.

Your Grade Point Average (GPA) or standardised test scores

While there's no clear-cut rule that dictates when to include your GPA, most career experts say to only keep it on a resume if it's over 3.5.

Once you have 2-3 years of work experience, it is time to remove your GPA from your resume. At this point in life, your work experience speaks more to your skills than your old GPA.

Your Mensa membership

Is there anything to be gained by pointing out that you have an exceptionally high intelligence quotient (IQ)? Or will it only communicate that yours is higher than the person reviewing your portfolio? It's probably best to leave it out.

Your zodiac sign

While it may be true that the best UX designers have the star sign Virgo like me, keep it out of your portfolio.

7. STORYTELLING WITH CASE STUDIES

Case studies form the bedrock of a UX portfolio. If there are no case studies, it's not a UX portfolio.

Why case studies?

Hiring is a gruelling and time-consuming process. No manager starts recruiting for fun. They need somebody to help meet a business objective or solve a problem. That's where case studies come in.

Case studies provide credible evidence of how you apply your expertise in the real world and how you helped a previous employer or client achieve their stated business objectives. Case studies are an excellent way of showing a hiring manager how good you are at your work.

Case studies appear to be less about sales and more about education or information. Their purpose is to sell, but not directly. Dealing in specifics rather than in claims or generalities, they're the written equivalent of an in-person demonstration.

If the case study works, it warms up your prospect, overcomes their objections, and answers initial questions about what you do and how well you do it. Ideally, portfolio reviewers should be able to relate to the problems you describe and understand the value of your solutions.

Case studies also allow you to be original. They can distinguish you from competitors and give you a way to stand out in the crowd.

Snupps 1/3

Designing a mobile app that investors felt happy to literally buy into.

☐ iPhone ☐ iPad ☐ Responsive web

The brief

Snupps is a London-based startup. They had an unreleased personal inventory app for the iPhone and iPad that they were concerned wouldn't show enough promise to investors. I was asked to improve both the app and their design process.

What I did

Tactical changes to the app
Snupps had promised potential investors that the app would be in the hands of beta testers by a specified date. To deliver on time, I reviewed the app for general usability and how well it supported key user tasks. My review revealed the app was over-complicated. In one case there were five ways of carrying out a single task. I worked directly with developers to remove, organise and hide elements as necessary. I also replaced interactions that were more commonplace on the web with native Apple iOS patterns.

Improving the design process
I interviewed stakeholders and team members to learn how they were currently working. These conversations coupled with observation revealed that inter-team communication needed to be improved for the talented team to work more efficiently. There was also a lot of unneeded documentation. Previous UX consultants had wireframed three or more alternative solutions before formally involving the development team and key stakeholders.

Moving forward, I included developers and stakeholders earlier in the process and sketched out the results of our collaboration instead. I then paired with the company's two user interface designers to update the app's user interface. The result was faster delivery with less room for error.

Long-term UX strategy
Once we had launched the beta application, I worked with the Snupps team to refine it further based on AppSee app analytics. We also optimised our design process further by reducing interaction differences between the iPhone and iPad versions of the app and establishing design patterns that we would reuse. Following the official release of the app, we also made changes to support future growth of the app into a full-blown social network.

Key tools and deliverables

- Sketching
- Workshops
- Pair design
- Flinto
- AppSee

Results

Team output increased. We met delivery dates. Three months following launch, the app was rated 5/5 by users.

Apple selected Snupps as an iTunes Best New Productivity App. It was also a finalist for Top Social App of 2014 at the Mobile Entertainment Awards.

More importantly for Snupps, investors approved of the application, and the company secured $5 million (£3 million) of seed capital.

118

Figure 7.1 One of my own case studies

How long should a case study be?

My research with hiring managers revealed that they don't want a blow-by-blow account of the entire design process for every previous project. What they want are stories.

Some marketers say a shorter case study is better. Others proclaim the benefits of long-form content. Writer Debbie Weil says a reasonable word count is 500 words[49]:

> "If your readers can't skim quickly to get the gist, you're wasting your efforts."

I say you should avoid writing a manual that will enable the portfolio reviewer to replicate your case study results on their own. The more information you provide, the more likely the reader will try to second-guess what you did and be critical of your actions and decisions. So, aim to provide just enough information and detail to demonstrate your value and nothing more. Definitely no more than 2000 words per case study. That's four pages of A4.

A framework may be helpful

Case studies are popular in business, particularly with highly-paid consultancies, who like to develop their own acronyms. Academia likes frameworks too. Consequently, there are quite a few.

• PAR: Problem, Action, Result

• CAR: Context, Action, Result

• SCR: Situation, Complication, Resolution

• STAR: Situation, Task, Action, Results

• CART: Context, Action, Result, Tools

• SAFE: Situation, Action/Activity, Findings, Effect

---

[49] https://www.marketingprofs.com/2/weil2.asp

- SOAR: Situation, Objective, Action, Results
- SOARA: Situation, Objective, Action, Results, Aftermath

I won't explain any of these frameworks in greater detail, but a quick Google should reap dividends. Any of these would be acceptable to use for a UX portfolio. Feel free to roll a die.

Thank you, Aristotle

Most frameworks lead back to the three-act story structure attributed to the Greek philosopher and polymath Aristotle:

- Setup: Introduction of the characters and the setting
- Confrontation: The characters encounter a challenge
- Resolution: The characters either triumphantly solve the problem or succumb to it.

It may help you to think of your case study as a story organised in this way.

Case study walk-through

Let me take you through the main sections of a case study built the framework I use myself:

- The brief
- What I did
- Results
- Tools and methods

The brief

This initial section describes your employer or client's problem, challenge, or opportunity and what you were asked to do.

It doesn't need to be lengthy, but it's crucial that you establish the context of the story, the customer, the industry, and the environment.

Be sure to give the reviewer a sense of scale. Explain who your client is and why they are notable. Consider location, market position, annual revenue, or the number of employees. Anything that elevates them. Don't assume people will know why a company is notable. It won't harm to state the obvious.

Having described your client and their standing, explain what they wanted to achieve. Was it to save X? Or increase Y? Did they have a negative consequence they wanted to overcome? A positive result they needed to obtain?

Try to convey the stakes involved. A good question to ask is, 'So what?' The answer should reveal why the problem, challenge, or opportunity meant something. However, when dealing with a negative situation, keep the tone positive.

So, if you were asked to look at the checkout flow, explain why. If a negative prefix with a positive, e.g. "Though business was strong, ACME felt their checkout flow could be optimised further and called me in to help."

Try and summarise the context in 2-3 sentences. It is easy to become over-descriptive, so practise summarising the context succinctly using only relevant information.

A template to help

This simple template will help you focus on the correct information to share. But rewrite the results, so your case studies seem less formulaic.

[Client] is [who they are and why they are notable].

They [the problem].

They asked me to [task you were given].

For example:

Tesco PLC is the world's third-largest retailer.

They commissioned a third-party review that concluded that Tesco's overall e-commerce UX performance was 'mediocre.'

They asked me to work with their digital teams to develop new design processes, standards, and metrics that would address any underlying problems.

What I did

This section provides a high-level walkthrough of how you addressed the business problem, challenge, or opportunity described in the brief. If you are a researcher, you might detail the methods you used and why.

Consider including:

• The problems you discovered.
• How you discovered them.
• The challenges you faced.
• How you addressed them.
• Key milestones.
• Any key or big 'aha' moments

Be clear about your role

You must communicate the particular skills you brought to bear on your selected project.

It's equally important to show how you work with others. Hiring managers notice when you use 'I' or 'We.' However, be sure who 'We' are is evident to the reader.

Provide the why

Support every statement. Explain every decision unless it's a hypothesis. Explain why you chose to use a specific tool or method. This is what hiring managers mean when they say they want to see a candidate's thinking.

Remember that you are not the user. My research revealed many boot camp graduate portfolios containing phrases like 'The navigation is confusing to users..." that lacked supporting evidence. If it's only your opinion, admit it.

Use subheadings to maintain interest

While the heading 'What I did' will get people in the door, good subheadings encourage readers to stick around and engage with the detail.

The subheadings should demand attention and provide an overview of the following paragraphs. For example, 'Shrinking the product development cycle helps us move to market faster' is more interesting than 'Our product development cycle.'

The results

As brand consultant Tate Linden says, 'Good designers are praised for their technique. Great designers for their impact.'

So, this is where you describe the results of your hard work for your client. Did your employer or client get the desired outcome expressed in the brief? Did you achieve what you had set out to achieve?

Questions to consider:

- How has the client benefited from your work?
- What were the immediate benefits?
- What are the longer-term benefits?
- What do you expect the longer-term benefits to be?

If possible, use hard numbers. Give a percentage if your employer or client would prefer you didn't.

If you don't have metrics, use a testimonial. How did your employer or client feel about your work and the results? Get a direct quote articulating your contributed value.

Once projects have been delivered, keep an eye out for company annual reports, press coverage and the like. If the work was significant, it might well be mentioned - and you can reuse this material.

Reflection / What you learned

Some case studies follow the results with the designer's reflections on the project or a summary of their recommended next steps. My interviews with hiring managers suggested that they were split on the importance of including this. I suspect it has more value for designers early on in their careers.

If you wish to include your reflections, consider:

- What worked? What didn't? Why?
- What would you have done differently had you more time or more knowledge at the beginning?
- What surprised you? What did you learn?
- How will you use that knowledge in the future?

Tools and methods

Clients often give recruiters specific things to look for, so it can be helpful to them if you include a list of the tools and methods you used during a project.

Don't limit this list to software applications, and don't include everyday applications such as Microsoft Office or Google Apps. Hiring managers will assume you know these. Research methods to consider adding:

- Usability testing
- Contextual enquiry
- Participatory design
- User interviews
- Remote usability testing
- Pop-up usability testing
- Diary studies
- A/B testing

- Online surveys
- Stakeholder interviews
- Stakeholder workshops
- Competitor analysis
- Analytics review
- Heuristic review
- Eye tracking
- Task analysis

Tools:

- Figma
- Sketch
- InVision
- Axure RP
- HTML prototyping
- SurveyMonkey

- Optimal Workshop
- UsabilityHub
- UserTesting.com
- Iterate
- Optimizely
- Loop11

Design methods:

- Personas
- Content inventory
- Content audit

- User interface design
- Storyboarding
- Mental models

Project frameworks:

- Scrum
- Lean UX
- Design sprints
- Kanban

This is not an exhaustive list. List anything that you believe a recruiter would be looking for.

Highlights and sidebars

Case studies are great tools to provide an overview of past performance, but they provide little opportunity for you to emphasise specific skills or areas of interest to hiring managers. That's where highlights and sidebars come in.

Highlights and sidebars allow you to draw a portfolio reviewer's attention to the areas that you want their focus on. They're essentially deep dives into specific parts of the project you wish to emphasise.

You can use highlights to address essential vacancy requirements:

- If they are looking for a team player, highlight a specific time you worked successfully with people. Workshop facilitation, pair designing, etc.
- Suppose they are looking for a leader. Detail when you took the lead. Mentoring, facilitation, supervision, etc.
- If they are looking for somebody who thrives in a fast-paced environment, illustrate how you juggled several projects simultaneously.
- If they are looking for somebody creative, walk through a particularly innovative solution.

You can also use highlights to draw a portfolio reviewer's attention to work activities that you wish to do more of. For example, if you are a product designer who would like to do more research, you can use highlights to draw attention to the research you have completed to date, even if it has played only a small part in each of the projects you feature.

Ideas to consider

• Original research — what you discovered during a project.

• A user's perspective — how your solution changed their world for the better.

• A deep explanation of some aspect of the design.

• A key obstacle and how you overcame it.

• An 'aha' moment and why it was so significant.

• A walkthrough of a specific interaction.

• Testimonials — how colleagues found working with you.

• A photo story walking through the design process.

• A key artefact (or artifact) explained in detail.

• A simple story about some aspect of your previous work.

Some highlight examples from my own portfolio follow.

Snupps 2/3

☐ iPhone ☐ iPad ☐ Responsive web

How we designed Snupps

1. Sketching
Sketching individually on paper or collaboratively on a whiteboard improved communication, reduced errors, and allowed us to deliver changes quicker.

2. Pair design
I've been pair designing since 2006. It's an easy way to increase efficiency, effectiveness, and morale in teams.

3. Prototype and test.
We tried various prototyping tools before settling on Flinto for its faithful replication of native iOS transitions. Following delivery, we reviewed AppSee app analytics daily.

What Snupps thought

"Ian made highly noticeable contributions to our delivery processes but more importantly to our end product during his tenure with Snupps. He is a consummate professional and brings rich experience to the job. It was a pleasure to work with Ian."
—Arthur Holcombe, Managing Director

"Ian's extensive experience and top-level design skills were a huge asset to us. He streamlined the design process and produced excellent work. Always open to challenge and new ideas, he maximised the quality of his solutions without compromise to timescales and maintained focus where firmness was required."
—Richard Green, Delivery Manager

"Ian's one of the most knowledgeable UX professionals I know. He's highly approachable, a good listener and keen to help others. I consider him a mentor of the design team, giving us plenty of advice and challenging us to perform better. He's incredibly committed and a wonderful person to work with."
—Bruno Martins, Lead UI Designer

Figure 7.2 Photo story / Testimonials

128

Snupps 3/3

☐ iPhone   ☐ iPad   ☐ Responsive web

An example of effective mentoring

Philip was one of the user interface designers I managed at Snupps. When I arrived, he was at a low ebb. He preferred to fire off instant messages to the developers in the room next door, and face to face conversation often resulted in raised voices. Developers told me they felt he was obsessed with detail to the point of missing the big picture. On the other hand, I saw raw talent. I needed to take Philip under my wing.

Over the coming months, I coached Philip on how to present his designs and collaborate with others. I also worked with the wider Snupps team to arrange opportunities for Philip to step up and show his work.

The coaching worked. How do I know?

Philip is now their Lead Product Designer.

Figure 7.3 A simple story

129

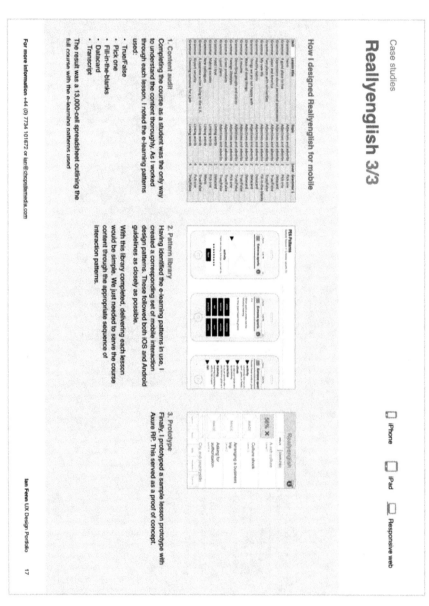

Figure *7.4 Design* process walk-through (photo story)

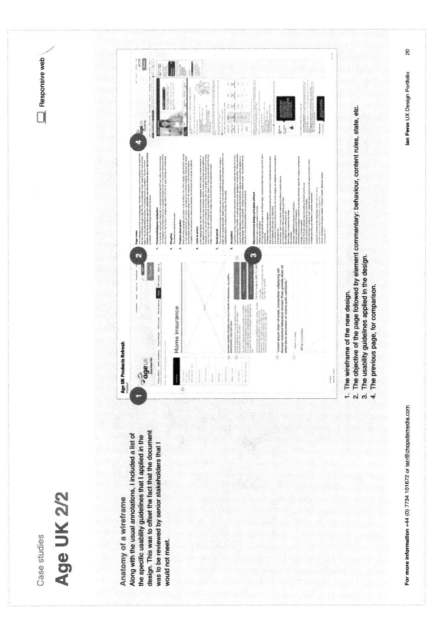

Case studies

Age UK 2/2

Anatomy of a wireframe

Along with the usual annotations, I included a list of the specific usability guidelines that I applied in the design. This was to offset the fact that the document was to be reviewed by senior stakeholders that I would not meet.

1. The wireframe of the new design.
2. The objective of the page followed by element commentary: behaviour, content rules, state, etc.
3. The usability guidelines applied in the design.
4. The previous page, for comparison.

Figure 7.5 A key artefact explained

131

Virgin Media 2/2

Designing for call centre agents
My field trips to call centres revealed that designing for call centre staff isn't quite the same as designing for most people.

Call centre agents are expert users. We often design for the beginner and accommodate the expert. Call centre applications need to be designed for experts and support the novice.

The user experience isn't limited to call centre agents. There is a caller unknowingly directing the action. The application needs to satisfy and accommodate the needs of both agent and caller. The application should also facilitate the agent sounding confident on every call.

Call centre staff often use multiple applications that work in different ways. If you are designing only one application, try to integrate with the others.

Agents are often under management pressure to meet a performance target. So, the application must facilitate personal performance goals in addition to organisational ones.

I also observed that Virgin Media agents would read retention offers to callers from a single sheet of paper, which there were no plans to remove. If they found the application less usable than this piece of paper, it would fail. This fact was instrumental in persuading stakeholders to prioritise agent and customer needs.

For more information +44 (0) 7734 101672 or ian@chopsifamedia.com

1. Retention offers. This is the sheet of paper the application needed to replace.

2. Calculator to manually calculate the total cost of bundles and add-ons.

3. Pad for scribbling down any information provided by the caller.

Figure 7.6 Original research

8. COMPLETING THE PICTURE

Most UX portfolios I've reviewed contain only an introduction and a collection of case studies. It's a good start, but adding further information can set you aside from competitors.

You can also use some of the ideas in this chapter to help you move forward into an area you have less experience in.

Additional Projects

A limitation of portfolios is that they only present a limited selection of work. If a client doesn't see exactly what they're looking for, you may not be added to a hiring manager's shortlist.

On the other hand, prospective employers or clients rarely provide enough information for candidates to fully optimise a portfolio.

So, this section is my attempt to address that issue, offering several short case studies of around 50 words each.

Figure 8.1 Additional projects example

Training and Education

After case studies, education is one of the most critical sections to have in your portfolio. Undertaking training demonstrates interest and enthusiasm for your chosen field.

You can also use training to unlock an area in which you have yet to gain professional experience. Suppose you are looking to move from one area of design to another. Complete courses in the new field and highlight them within this section. For example, if you are looking to move from research to design, list the design courses you have completed. A hiring manager is sure to be impressed.

If you are a recent UXD graduate, explain what you learned (and achieved) during your course so that hiring managers understand they are not starting with someone green.

If you are a more experienced practitioner who has completed many classes, list the courses grouped into topics to demonstrate a breadth of knowledge.

Otherwise, highlight the training you think will be most attractive to the portfolio reviewers.

Don't scan your certificates into your portfolio, one per page. I've seen this, and it's unnecessary. A description of the training you completed is more helpful to a hiring manager than the certificates you obtained.

Awards and honours

Awards indicate that previous employers, peers or others — those awarding the prize — valued your work. Formal recognition suggests a high level of skill and a strong work ethic.

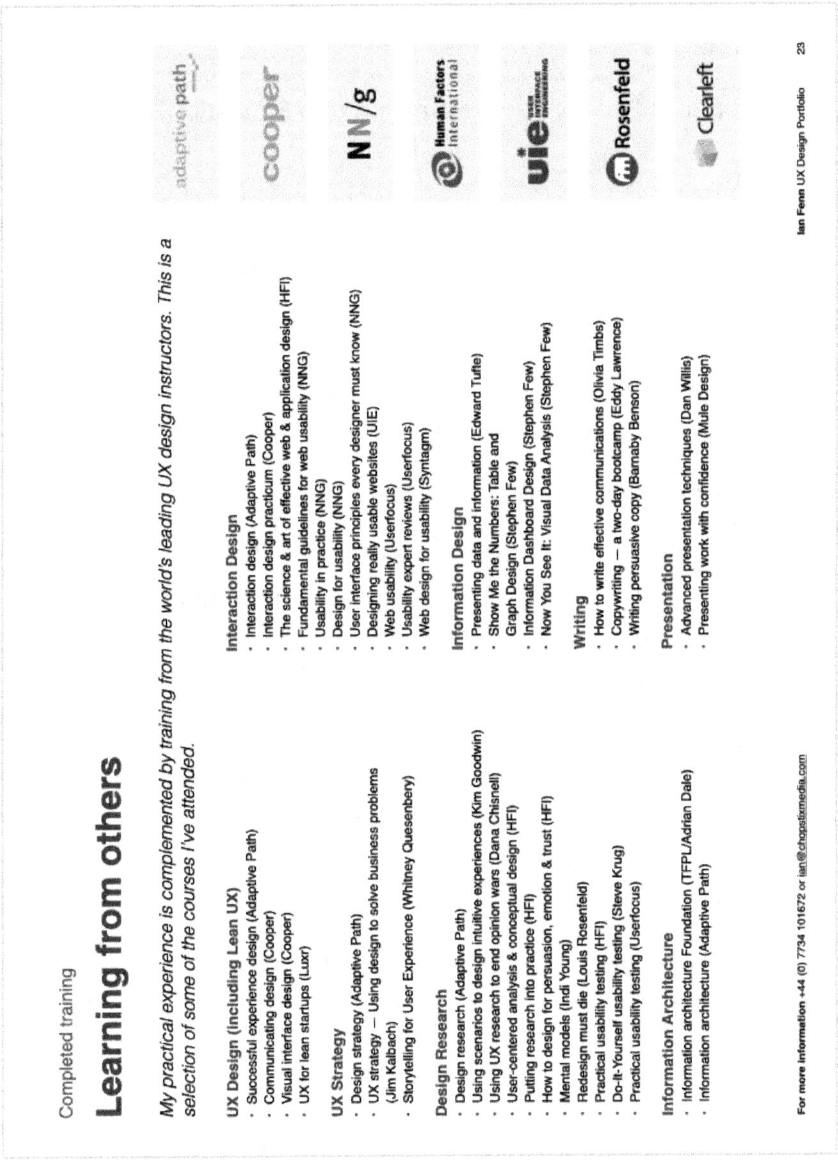
Completed training
Learning from others
My practical experience is complemented by training from the world's leading UX design instructors. This is a selection of some of the courses I've attended.
UX Design (including Lean UX)
· Successful experience design (Adaptive Path)
· Communicating design (Cooper)
· Visual interface design (Cooper)
· UX for lean startups (Luxr)
UX Strategy
· Design strategy (Adaptive Path)
· UX strategy — Using design to solve business problems (Jim Kalbach)
· Storytelling for User Experience (Whitney Quesenbery)
Design Research
· Design research (Adaptive Path)
· Using scenarios to design intuitive experiences (Kim Goodwin)
· Using UX research to end opinion wars (Dana Chisnell)
· User-centered analysis & conceptual design (HFI)
· Putting research into practice (HFI)
· How to design for persuasion, emotion & trust (HFI)
· Mental models (Indi Young)
· Redesign must die (Louis Rosenfeld)
· Practical usability testing (HFI)
· Do-It-Yourself usability testing (Steve Krug)
· Practical usability testing (Userfocus)
Information Architecture
· Information architecture Foundation (TFPL/Adrian Dale)
· Information architecture (Adaptive Path)
Interaction Design
· Interaction design (Adaptive Path)
· Interaction design practicum (Cooper)
· The science & art of effective web & application design (HFI)
· Fundamental guidelines for web usability (NNG)
· Usability in practice (NNG)
· Design for usability (NNG)
· User interface principles every designer must know (NNG)
· Designing really usable websites (UIE)
· Web usability (Userfocus)
· Usability expert reviews (Userfocus)
· Web design for usability (Syntagm)
Information Design
· Presenting data and information (Edward Tufte)
· Show Me the Numbers: Table and Graph Design (Stephen Few)
· Information Dashboard Design (Stephen Few)
· Now You See It: Visual Data Analysis (Stephen Few)
Writing
· How to write effective communications (Olivia Timbs)
· Copywriting — a two-day bootcamp (Eddy Lawrence)
· Writing persuasive copy (Barnaby Benson)
Presentation
· Advanced presentation techniques (Dan Willis)
· Presenting work with confidence (Mule Design)
adaptive path
cooper
NN/g
Human Factors International
uie
Rosenfeld
Clearleft
For more information +44 (0) 7734 101672 or ian@chopstixmedia.com
Ian Fenn UX Design Portfolio
23

Figure 8.2 Training and Education example

If you have a list of awards, I'm jealous. Please create a page for them, preferably with a photo of you or your team collecting the gong. If you have one or two awards, add them to the relevant case studies.

Add academic honours to the Training and Education section.

Patents

Patents are valuable. Companies, universities, and individuals make money from them. Startups actively try to create value by registering them. For example, Nest's ownership of patents was considered a significant driver for why Google purchased them in 2014. So, if you have been granted patents, it may make sense to have a section dedicated to listing and summarising them.

Speaking engagements / Talks

Employers like active industry speakers. People who present well are often singled out for leadership roles. Contributing to industry conferences portrays you as a thought leader and an educator of your peers. Hiring managers will consider that you have expertise in your field and are passionate about the industry.

If you have a presentation that you believe will strongly resonate with the portfolio reviewer, lead the section with a short talk description. Include past attendee numbers and positive comments from attendees.

Otherwise, list the title of each of your presentations and where they occurred. Embed or link to online slide decks or videos of the exhibitions where possible.

In my portfolio, I present two presentations that support my overall narrative. They also have links to videos of the talks too.

Sharing knowledge

I have spoken at a number of conferences including SXSW, Big Design, Midwest UX, UX Poland, UX Scotland, and UXLx. My talks are known for being practical and pragmatic. These are two of the most popular:

Getting UX done

If there's one problem UX designers are familiar with, it's the problem of getting their designs implemented – a 2012 survey of practitioners revealed the number one reason usability problems go unfixed is that the solution conflicts with the decision maker's belief or opinion.

After switching from creative producer to UX consultant, I was no longer responsible for deciding whether or not to implement a design.

At first I put my faith in the facts, hoping that decision makers would buy in to those. It wasn't enough. Then I tried collaboration techniques to get everyone on the same page. I found these don't always work either.

This humorous talk reveals how I threw together a mixture of psychology research and conjuring techniques to get more of my work implemented as I felt it should be.

☐ http://chopstix.it/guxd

Designing a UX portfolio

UX Portfolio required: three words that fill UX designers, new and experienced, with dread. Designers are often experts at telling their client's story, but find it difficult to communicate their own.

I used to be a portfolio skeptic, believing they caused more problems than they solved. But I'm also a pragmatist, and with requests from recruiters increasing, I set about creating the perfect UX portfolio. Since publication, copies have been requested by recruitment agents – not in relation to work, but to show to other designers as an example of how to do things right.

During this session I share my UX portfolio template and the thinking behind it so other UX designers can effectively represent their skills and experience to prospective employers and clients.

☐ http://chopstix.it/uievs

Speaking at UX Poland

Feedback from attendees

"You rewired my brain!", "Full of practical advice", "a really insightful and very frank talk", "Brilliant!!", "Inspiring!", "Awesome".

For more information +44 (0) 7734 101672 or ian@chopstixmedia.com

Figure 8.3 Speaking engagements / Talks example

Volunteer work

A 2016 Deloitte study of over 2,500 hiring managers in the USA revealed that 82% prefer candidates with volunteer experience. 92% also said volunteer activities build leadership skills.[50]

Include it if you feel your volunteer work is relevant to your UX career goal. But don't get carried away and load your portfolio with every good deed. Be selective.

Treat your volunteer work much as you have your case studies. Ensure you spell out what you achieved. Quantify your accomplishments. For example, if you co-founded a local UX event, explain how you planned it and how many attendees regularly turn up. Make it clear that it was a significant amount of responsibility.

Some career advisors believe that job applicants should avoid highlighting volunteering related to religion, politics, and sexual orientation. I'm afraid I have to disagree. If your volunteer work is essential to you, why would you even want to be considered by an employer that would discriminate against you for it? (If a company discriminates against you, it's their loss.)

Activities and Interests

As we've discussed, hiring managers want to know that you can do the job but also want to feel that they want you to do it. They will be looking for an indication of how rounded you are as a person and how well you will fit in with future colleagues. Activities and interests can help here.

Activities and interests can also differentiate you from other applicants and introduce topics for discussion at the interview. Interviewers always mention that I trained as a professional

---

[50] http://fortune.com/2016/06/28/volunteer-work-resume/

Chinese chef when they read my portfolio in advance. It's how I know they have read it.

Professionally-relevant interests

Examples of professionally relevant interests include writing, photography, and coding in the UX design field. They are excellent skills for a UX designer to have.

Amateur theatrical work or singing in a band is also relevant - both indicate creativity and confidence — crucial when applying for a role that includes facilitating workshops, mentoring and handling stakeholders.

Non-professional activities

Non-professional activities would include working part-time behind a bar or in a shop, which suggests an interest in people. Studying abroad counts too. It indicates an interest in engaging with the world as a whole. These are admirable traits for a user-centred designer.

How to choose what to highlight

Don't go crazy and list every interest you have. Focus on the activities that you feel will interest your portfolio reviewers. But, do be honest. No shark-taming unless you did. Choose activities and interests that you love. Don't fabricate them. You won't explain them as enthusiastically or passionately, and the interview panel will be able to tell. Be prepared to show off your skills if asked. Also, be specific. For example, don't say 'reading' when you can say what you've been reading.

Writing and podcasting

Blogs have passed their peak but remain a valuable tool for business professionals to demonstrate their knowledge and expertise. Podcasts continue to grow in number and interest.

The key to success with both is to have a focus. General topics don't tend to lead to substantial audiences. So, avoid creating a general design blog. Try to narrow down your topic of interest to the point where it becomes different from what sites like UX Mastery[51] and UX Matters[52] do.

If you are new to UX design, document your journey to develop your skills. Hiring managers have advised me that they are interested in seeing this as it demonstrates commitment and interest.

If building a web-based portfolio, highlight the latest blog entries on your homepage underneath your critical case studies. List posts that you feel will resonate most with your intended portfolio reviewer for a PDF portfolio. For each entry, post the title, link, a short description and, if appropriate, the number of views and comments.

For more excellent distribution, re-publish your blog post to Medium[53] and LinkedIn[54] around two weeks later. Link to the original blog posts from the foot of the new copy.

---

[51] https://uxmastery.com/

[52] https://www.uxmatters.com/

[53] https://medium.com/

[54] https://linkedin.com/

Client testimonials

Most of your portfolio is written from your perspective. Client testimonials allow you to have others reinforce your claims.

There are things that other people have more licence to say. For example, describing yourself as a 'UX thought leader' will seem big-headed, but not if a former client or colleague says it for you.

Present edited highlights from the LinkedIn testimonials you gathered after reading Chapter 4. You can also plunder your performance reviews for suitable comments if you are an employee.

What clients think of working with me

For further testimonials visit https://uk.linkedin.com/in/ifenn

"Ian is **an exceptional UX practitioner**, balancing the business requirements with the user's needs to produce an intuitive experience and functional design. Ian's analytical and detailed approach was key to a number of recent projects, guiding their direction and **producing some great results.**"

- Peter Lambert, Head of UX, Global Personals

"Ian was **invaluable** at BT, bringing **in-depth expertise** in online user experience to the team as well as a passion for all things internet. His efforts went well beyond normal hours as he invested personal time to investigate opportunities to improve the site and ensuring his thinking was up-to-date by networking with other experts."

- David Morgan, Head of Online Business, BT plc

"Ian joined us to help develop a web application for a new insurance proposition. He brought with him **an abundance of usability knowledge** and expertise which he was more than happy to share. This enabled us to work collaboratively **increasing our in-house knowledge** as well as him producing some first class outputs. He has great attention to detail and showed great flexibility in producing top notch work in a climate of incomplete and changing requirements."

- Christian Young, Lead User Experience Architect, AVIVA plc

"Ian is a **hard working and dedicated** usability and interaction design expert. At Virgin Media he worked tirelessly to champion the user, always thinking creatively around business requirements to achieve the best experience possible. His work is backed up by **a wealth of experience** both in user interface design and in front end development, and I would welcome the opportunity to work with him again."

- Kirsty Brown, User Experience Manager, Virgin Media

"Ian is a highly focused and hardworking individual who offers a **wealth of knowledge** particularly in the areas of user experience and accessibility. Ian is an **innovative thinker** and is able to bring fresh thinking to any project. Given the opportunity, I would happily employ Ian again in the future."

- Llan Brook-Tyler, Head of Site, BT plc

"Having worked with Ian for over 3 years I've really valued his support and learnt from his **depth of knowledge** and understanding of the internet industry. His commitment to placing the customer at the heart of everything he does is unquestionable, as is his desire to provide an optimal, accessible user experience for all."

- Martin Faux, Head of BT Broadband Office, BT plc

"Ian is **dedicated to delivering the simplest solution possible** and always keeping the core customer need the focus of the experience, resulting in **quality, intuitive interface and functionality design.**"

- Richard Edwards, Digital Planning Director, LIDA

"With his unique mix of journalistic and broadcasting experience, Ian developed **compelling, content-driven solutions that were a perfect fit** for our broadcast clients. Ian is a great web copywriter and is also very visually oriented; he understands what works from the end-user's perspective, what "sells" and how to develop content that is engaging and immersive. Ian **always brings fresh thinking to projects and has an entrepreneurial attitude that keeps him focused on the end results.** I would wholeheartedly recommend Ian for any senior interactive production or management position."

- Adrian Tennant, Managing Director, Alchemy Digital

Linked in

Figure 8.4 Client testimonials example

144

Thank You / Next Steps

As we discussed in Chapter 5, your contact details (or a link to them) should be on every page of your portfolio. So, you may consider having a 'Thank you or 'Next Steps' page to be redundant. However, they can prove an effective way of getting your personality across, as this example from website design and development agency Jabberwokie[55] indicates.

Figure 8.5 Jabberwokie thank you page

What not to include in your portfolio

There are a few things I've seen in UX portfolios that resonate poorly with hiring managers. This is not an exhaustive list.

---

55 https://www.jabberwokie.com/

UX managers on junior UX portfolios

"Anything that demonstrates their interests and abilities count. Theoretical pieces, hackday stuff, personal homepage, hobby stuff, blogging, etc., show they're self-motivated with a curiosity and passion for this field. A portfolio consisting only of academic assignments can give the impression of someone whose heart is not really in it." — Francois Jordaan

"I would look for a wide variety of work that gave evidence of competence, their general attitude, willingness to learn, and what they love doing. Demonstrating learning, blogging and participating in hack days is really important because that means they are willing to get off their assess and contribute, learn and try things out." —James Chudley

"For a junior, I don't care if it's real work or work that they have produced for their studies. I like seeing images of work on the wall as that's the way I like to work. It means they're used to working collaboratively." — Angel Brown

"It's about the narrative. If they have a story to tell about the way they do the work they do (which they should!), then construct a portfolio around that narrative. I really don't care about the level of fidelity in a UX portfolio. I care about how you went about it. I'm not going to read an awful lot." — Tim Caynes

"When you meet talented UXers you can just tell. They'll be on twitter.They'll have photos of them holding a mic and pointing at screens.They will have attended hackathons...You can tell the good ones from a conversation - they already want to change the world. — Dug Falby

How you get into UX

Everybody has a story about getting into UX, but most hiring managers suggest saving it for the interview.

What I love about working in UX

The portfolio indicates how you will meet the viewer's needs, not yours.

Resume / CV

Hiring managers expect the resume or CV to be a separate document if your portfolio is a PDF.

If you want to include it, add it to the end of the PDF and keep the page orientation the same.

9. DEALING WITH COMMON CONSTRAINTS

Limited work

If you're starting your career, take a deep breath. All the hiring managers I interviewed described making allowances for somebody early in their career. But that doesn't mean you shouldn't give it your best shot.

With new practitioners, good hiring managers - those you want to work with - are looking for folks with a passion for UX and a desire to learn. If you have only one case study, supplement it with links to your blog posts and other elements demonstrating these qualities.

If you are starting, your work history will be limited. Don't fret. Everyone has to start somewhere.

Good hiring managers like to see the following when recruiting for a junior role:

• enthusiasm for UX design

• curiosity about people and technology

• ability to learn quickly

• attention to detail

• a willingness to receive constructive criticism and develop off the back of it - in practice, this means evidence of teamwork and collaboration

So, take a deep breath and relax - the best hiring managers will allow for a candidate's lack of experience when reviewing a portfolio. One case study could be enough if it's a good one and complemented by other material that emphasises the personal qualities they are looking for.

If you have a limited work history, you can complete your portfolio in several ways.

Do a course

Many short-term courses in UX design encourage participants to create a case study as they work through the syllabus. These are a good option if you can afford the fees, particularly when you consider that some institutions also hold end-of-course meet-ups with potential employers.

Ensure you thoroughly research any course you're considering. Ask yourself the following questions:

- Does the syllabus involve completing a project that can serve as a portfolio case study?
- Does it have a good reputation?
- Does the lead instructor have plenty of industry and teaching experience?
- Is the course accompanied by a certificate of attendance or a certification?
- Is it worth the money?

Offer a non-profit help

But what if you have limited work? What do you do? The best answer is sadly the flippant one: get some more. Contact a voluntary organisation. Offer to complete research or design for them. Develop their content strategy. Do something. Treat it like a paid project.

A professional designer should never work free of charge, but there's no issue in donating your skills to a non-profit or charity you believe in. Think of a cause you have an affinity for and offer to help where you can. Handle the project professionally, treating your time as necessary a currency as money. Document your process as you go, and you should have a great case study with an appreciative client.

Do a hackathon

Another option, if you have a limited work history, is to attend hack days. There is usually an abundance of software engineers and a need for more researchers, designers, or writers at most events. The time constraint and pressure are real. Write the experience up.

Hackathons offer designers a quick way to generate a case study. These short-term events, also known as hack days, bring together developers and others to work intensively on software or hardware projects. Companies often organise hackathons to encourage product development, but local community groups also arrange hackathons to address a government or non-profit cause.

In addition to obtaining portfolio material, you will meet potential contacts who may pass work your way later.

Hackathons often last a day or an entire weekend. They begin with presentations that set the tone and explain the project brief to the participants. After the talks, participants will divide into groups and start working on their solutions to the problem posed.

These events compress a product development cycle into just a few hours, so everyone is working under pressure and fuelled by coffee and pizza. Take jelly beans.

Make up a project

This is the most common option chosen by junior designers. If you adopt this approach, there are a few guidelines to ensure you get the most out of it.

First, avoid contributing to 'the dribbblisation of design'. (fn) The concern here is that the dribble community praises and promotes simple design work intended to impress fellow members rather than address real business issues. If you're going to make up a project for your portfolio, try to solve a real problem.

Secondly, ensure the project is as realistic as possible by considering real-world constraints. In January 2010, Tyler Thompson redesigned the Delta Air Lines boarding pass. It was a gorgeous design with one problem - implementing it would require Delta to replace over 10,000 printers situated at airports around the globe to handle new typography and colour requirements. Take the time to research and factor in real-world constraints - your design will be much stronger if it's practical.

Finally, be realistic in your scope of work. In other words, don't attempt to redesign LinkedIn in an afternoon, even if it appears that this is what the original company did.

Redesign

In February 2014, Francine Lee posted the first of a pair of articles about redesigning the photos experience of the cloud storage app Dropbox.[56] With its strong research focus, the article caught the attention of Dropbox themselves, and she joined the company three months later.

---

56 https://medium.com/bridge-collection/a-guerilla-usability-test-on-dropbox-photos-e6a1e37028b4

Despite Francine's success, boldly suggesting changes to a prospective employer or client's product is not without risk. Some companies may respond well to having their product analysed or redesigned. Others may not. Anticipate the response before you go to the trouble of learning directly. Study as much as possible about the client and their business - an unsolicited redesign will put your knowledge under the microscope and highlight just how little or much you know. If you go ahead with an unsolicited redesign, ensure it's the best work you can do.

Design contests

Don't, whatever you do, enter a design contest to beef up your portfolio. Theoretical work has a long-term damaging effect on the design industry. Don't work for free. Try one of the other ideas instead.

Design contest websites promise clients 'dozens of unique designs in just a week'. The site invites designers to provide work to a brief so that they will receive payment if their work is selected. Most participants are just a form of speculative work where they are guaranteed to lose out.

Looking to move from another role

Are you looking to move into UX from an unrelated role? That's a toughie. It's far easier to transition to a UX role within the same company than it is to do it by changing jobs.

Transferring from one job to another is one of the most challenging things. It's often easiest to accomplish as an internal candidate. Get into a business in one role, then rally to move to the UX role you desire.

It's still possible to make a career change as an external candidate, but it's more challenging. To give it your best shot, write up your previous work as case studies and ensure you highlight your transferable skills throughout.

If you want to try, examine your previous work for UX methods. Write those projects up.

One loooooooong project

What if you've worked on the same product for a long time? The chances are that your work was broken into discrete projects, perhaps based on researching or adding new functionality. Try giving each significant development its case study.

First, break the long project into multiple case studies. Treat each new or updated feature as an individual achievement. Demonstrate plenty of variety in your work, even though you worked on the same project throughout. In other words, make it evident that you didn't just lazily do the same thing every year for several years.

Break a long project into multiple case studies like this.

Secondly, steal a few ideas from the previous section on limited work history and supplement your project experience with examples of hackathons, non-profit, or personal project work.

Work completed some time ago

There are situations such as returning to the industry after a period of leave - maternity leave, for example - when you may need to feature work you completed some time ago.

If this is the case, try to avoid drawing attention to the age of the case study:

• Remove any date stamps.

• Remove or reduce artefacts or images that look dated.

• If necessary, emphasise timeless design techniques the portfolio reviewer is likely familiar with.

Projects that didn't deliver

Projects that never deliver are a tough break. A friend once worked on a project for over a year, only for their employer to acquire a competing solution before anything launched. The project was closed down as a result. This isn't an uncommon occurrence in the corporate world. The likelihood is that the in-house project was a backup plan if the acquisition didn't go through.

Explaining what you did in situations like this may still be valuable. Even though the project didn't launch, a powerful testimonial from your employee or client may act as the case study result.

Finally, accept a virtual hug from me. You probably need it.

Non-disclosure agreements

Non-Disclosure Agreements, or Confidentiality Agreements, can cause designers considerable anxiety. A story is making the rounds of a designer who completed some work for a digital agency and placed it in his public portfolio. Shortly afterwards, the agency sued him for violating his confidentiality agreement. I have confirmed that this has happened at not one but two agencies. It's an experience none of us wishes to have.

Non-Disclosure Agreements (NDAs) are simply agreements between designers and clients that protect the client's confidential information.

Common suggestions debunked

Browse the web, and you will find many suggestions on how to deal with a Non-Disclosure Agreement. Some of these deserve debunking, so let's begin.

Break the NDA

Some designers adopt a 'devil may care attitude to Non-Disclosure Agreements and share their work regardless of what they have previously signed. Their thinking is that no company in their right mind will sue. Therefore, the risk is low.

While the likelihood of being sued for having personal work in your portfolio may be small, that's not the only risk.

Several of the hiring managers I've spoken with for this book have in the past received material clearly labelled private and confidential, which they feel they shouldn't have been given. In one case, a candidate sent a hiring manager a full copy of a financial organisation's yet-to-launch digital strategy with 'Commercially Sensitive. Not to be distributed outside the company.' stamped on every page. The hiring manager felt compromised, immediately rejected the candidate and informed the recruiter representing them to take more care in advising their clients in future.

So, breaking a Non-Disclosure Agreement and sharing confidential information in your portfolio will lead to many hiring managers wondering if you will do the same with their material. They'll question your ability to keep the confidence and be concerned about your professionalism in general. Just don't do it.

Restrict portfolio access with a password

Another suggestion often given online is to protect your portfolio with a password and only provide access to prospective employers and clients you have previously spoken with:

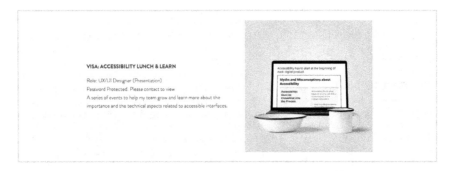

Figure 9.1 "Please contact for password" example

There are two issues with this approach. First, portfolio reviewers have an extra hurdle (entering the password) to jump before they can see any work. Secondly, you lose the opportunity to have a public portfolio, which you may need.

Password-based protection is beneficial only if it's only what the Non-Disclosure Agreement permits. If so, put the minds of portfolio reviewers at ease. State clearly that you have permission to include the material. 'Made available with permission.' is all you need to say.

A related suggestion to the password barrier is to ask people to contact you so you can go through confidential work in person:

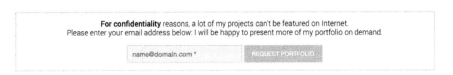

For **confidentiality** reasons, a lot of my projects can't be featured on Internet.
Please enter your email address below: I will be happy to present more of my portfolio on demand.

name@domain.com *   REQUEST PORTFOLIO

Figure 9.2 Password prompt example

Be careful. A message like this could suggest that you are willing to divulge commercially-sensitive information only if an email address is provided.

Anonymise the work

The most popular suggestion online for dealing with NDAs is to anonymise the work affected. This is rarely successful, as it is often possible to identify the client by cross-referencing the obfuscated design against information provided in an accompanying resume or CV.

Let's say you have an excellent e-learning case study in your portfolio. The client isn't named, and any identifying text has been redacted or removed. So far, so good. But then the hiring manager recalls your resume or CV, stating that you had previously worked for an e-learning company and who it was. They now know who the obfuscated work was produced for.

Anonymising work may not work if the client is listed in an accompanying resumé or curriculum vitae.

So, if you are going to anonymise work, you have to remove the client or employer's name from your resume or CV. But then you lose the value of including that company in your resume or CV, and who you've worked for is usually the main thing a recruiter or hiring manager is interested in.

What does work

So, what's a boy or girl to do? Well, we do have options.

Avoid signing a NDA in the first place

The ideal situation, of course, is to avoid signing an NDA in the first place.

Ask for company policy during the recruitment process. The best time to do this is not at your initial interview but after the company has been interested in hiring you. Ask them about their policy on employees sharing sketches, screenshots, wireframes and other deliverables in their portfolio.

If they reply that all work is subject to a Non-Disclosure Agreement, decide if it's a deal-breaker or if you want to ask for changes.

Review the NDA and understand what it allows

Always get a work contract reviewed by a lawyer. If this isn't an option, do take the time to review the document yourself. Don't just sign it. I've lost track of the number of employment contracts I've read over the past decade only to find a troublesome clause that the client subsequently claimed has never been a problem for anyone else.

I'm not entitled or insured to provide legal advice, but there are a few things I particularly look out for when I review a Non-Disclosure Agreement. Follow suit at your own risk.

Look at the definition of confidential information

Have they defined the information considered confidential by the agreement? Have they stated what the deal doesn't cover?

The limitation on use and disclosure

What, if anything, can you do with any of the information covered by the agreement? Your obligations as a recipient should be clear.

The term of agreement

What is the time limit of any obligations stated in the agreement? Until the project is made public by the employer or client? A year? Until you die?

Ask for the NDA to be amended

Once you've read the Non-Disclosure Agreement, you may wish to request permission to be able to:

* Mention the client in your resume or CV.

* Include work in your portfolio.

* Present the work to prospective clients in private.

You can request a time limit to any Non-Disclosure Agreement. A maximum of three years should be adequate for most employers or clients.

It is much harder to request permission later on, but that doesn't mean it isn't worth trying. Requesting approval to distribute a specific case study may be more successful than a general request to share deliverables and other documentation.

Share what you can share

Your final option is to share what you can share and nothing more. But what you can share is probably more than you think. Again, I'm not a lawyer, and this is not legal advice.

Non-Disclosure Agreements typically protect information that is not in the public domain. So, information the employer has released previously is not subject to disclosure.

If your employer or client has issued a press or media release about your project, you may be able to share the same information.

If your job description was published online, that's also public information - it should be safe for you to share that too.

Finally, see if you can write around your Non-Disclosure Agreement by summarising your design process without any commercially-sensitive detail.

Whatever you do, stay within the limitations of your Non-Disclosure Agreement.

Submit your work for a UX award

Product leader Michael Calleia suggests obtaining a company or client's agreement to submit their project for an award such as the IxDA Interaction Awards[57] or the UX Design Awards.[58] The award submission is public if the company agrees and can be shared within your portfolio.

Use your knowledge to solve a problem

If you're really restricted, another option is to ditch convention and create a portfolio of wisdom. Inside of serving up case studies, share short articles that detail how you would address common problems that a hiring manager would be interested in getting help with. For example:

- Growing a design team
- Implementing a design system
- Developing a brand identity
- Developing a research plan without access to users

---

[57] https://awards.ixda.org/

[58] https://ux-design-awards.com/

10. EVALUATING YOUR UX PORTFOLIO

Well done if you've reached this chapter after completing the first draft of your UX portfolio. Please accept a gold star.

You may be eager to share it with others. Please don't. At least, not yet. Do these simple things first.

Check your spelling

Check your spelling. Every portfolio I have read over the past three months has contained a typo or spelling error. While there can be safety in numbers, typos don't suggest you have the 'attention to detail' that employers frequently request.

Check your tone

I once read a portfolio that contained the following statement:

> The agency didn't win the account back for many reasons, but the design wasn't one of them (according to the client, and I doubt they would have gone out of their way to spare any feelings.)

> While the live site, unfortunately, shifted well away from the designs due to the project management process, the design thinking was sound.

Trash-taking colleagues, the client or their original product, is a definite red flag for hiring managers. Who wants to work with somebody like that?

Check that everything you have written is professional and upbeat. Save the negative stuff for your therapist or partner.

In particular, avoid blaming clients or employers for bad decisions. Portfolio reviewers could view such criticism as an example of your failure to persuade or do your job correctly.

We all lose arguments from time to time. Gracefully dealing with disappointment is part of the job.

If you need to mention that a stakeholder decision significantly affected a design, try presenting it as a constraint followed by a solution. For example:

> The project team could not interview users directly. So, I suggested we produce a modular design that we could rapidly amend in response to user feedback following the launch.

No profanity

Countless articles on the internet[59] argue that intelligent people swear and curse more, but leave it out of your portfolio. Avoid swearing in your social media accounts, particularly if they're linked to your online portfolio.

Edit with a highlighter

From copywriter Henneke Duistermaat comes a neat trick:[60] Highlight the essential words in your copy and work only with them.

Her example:

---

[59] https://theconversation.com/think-swearing-isnt-big-or-clever-think-again-71043

[60] http://www.enchantingmarketing.com/write-clear-and-concise-sentences/

> I will provide you with suggestions on your performance to overcome the challenges you encounter every day while working for a problematic boss so that you can feel less stressed.

Meaningful words in bold:

> I will provide you with **suggestions** on your performance so you can **overcome** the **challenges** you encounter **every day** while **working** for a **demanding boss**, so you can feel **less stressed**.

Henneke's clear and concise version:

> I help you overcome the daily challenges of working for a demanding boss, so you feel less stressed.

Read your writing aloud

Reading your UX portfolio aloud will help you identify sentences that may need to be simplified. If you take a breath in the middle of a sentence, the sentence is too long and could be simplified into two or more.

Also, it's your UX portfolio, not somebody else's. Your voice, or a professional variation, should be loud and clear. Write the way you talk. Don't write in the third person. Doing this makes you seem pretentious.

If it doesn't sound like you, edit or rewrite it until it does.

Use assistive technology

A spell checker will identify many typos but not misused words. For those, Digital Product Consultant Matt Goddard suggests having your computer read your portfolio text right back to you. Try VoiceOver[61] on the Mac or Narrator[62] on Windows.

Use my checklist

Based on my portfolio research with researchers, designers, recruiters, and hiring managers, I've created the following checklist. Have you omitted anything mentioned without good reason?

Have you:

- Identified the reviewers of your portfolio and their needs in terms of candidate experience?
- Curated a selection of realistic projects that demonstrate comparable work experience?
- Respected any non-disclosure agreement and privacy laws such as GDPR?
- Written the introduction to your portfolio so that it clearly articulates your value?
- Written your biography to convey what you can do for the reviewer, relevant experience, and your pleasant working nature?
- Written case study titles to summarise each chosen project?
- Checked that each case study is free of misspellings, typos, and poor grammar?
- Ensured that your portfolio is easy to navigate with no unnecessary interaction required.

For each case study, have you:

---

[61] https://www.apple.com/uk/accessibility/vision/

[62] https://support.microsoft.com/en-us/windows/complete-guide-to-narrator-e4397a0d-ef4f-b386-d8ae-c172f109bdb1

- Summarised your overall design process and given essential details such as project duration?
- Put the client into context: who they are and the business outcome they needed?
- Communicated your role and how you collaborated with others?
- Explained vital decisions and the thinking behind them?
- Presented an understanding of research and design activities, including when to use them?
- Explained the business impact of the project, next steps, and your key learnings?
- Structured the content so that it is quick to scan, with ample headings?
- Used relevant photographs, cut-away artefacts, and other visuals in preference to wordy blocks of text?

For a free printable copy of the checklist to check off, send your proof of book purchase to me at ian@uxnotes.com.

Ask a fellow professional

Online, I often see this:

Figure 10.1 The wrong way to ask for critique

People complete their portfolios and rush to their nearest social media group to tell everyone. "Can I have some feedback?" they ask.

Then, I see a variety of comments about the portfolio. The comments often contain unrelated and conflicting opinions. People from all stages of their design careers — career shifters, early-career designers, and senior designers — all chime in. I see praise and compliments among the opinions like, "I like your portfolio! It looks interesting and professional." Unfortunately, getting feedback this way rarely yields valuable input. It's hard to improve your portfolio when you receive conflicting, scattered feedback.

UX community groups don't seem to handle portfolio reviews much better. They often match portfolio owners with senior practitioners or recruiters, put them in a room and let them get on with it. Again, the advice is likely to be subjective and conflicting. So, what should you do?

The answer is to obtain portfolio critique, not feedback.

Handle portfolio critique as you would product critique.

If you are the portfolio owner

1. It's easy to spend two hours discussing a single case study, but few critique sessions last this long. So, spend some time up-front to decide precisely what you want feedback on. Work out where advice would be most helpful.
2. Print out your portfolio, even if it's online. It's easier and quicker to scribble notes onto a printout than to take notes digitally.
3. Start the critique by explaining who the portfolio is for, what you know about them and what you want them to think. Your goal is for people to adjust their thinking to a specific user's needs, so they share their best advice rather than their subjective opinion.

4. Then explain the kind of feedback you want. Alternatively, ask your reviewer (or reviewers), "Is the portfolio effective, given what I want the reader to think? Why or why isn't it effective?"

5. Now listen without judgment and make notes. Don't talk too much or get defensive. Remember: you are not your design, even if it's your portfolio. However, do ask clarifying questions if you need to.

6. End by saying thank you.

If you are a reviewer

1. Listen carefully to the context provided by the portfolio owner.

2. Put yourself in the target reader's shoes. Portfolio critique is not about your personal preferences.

3. Ask questions rather than make comments. "What was your reasoning here?" "What do you want the user to think at this point? "Have you considered [something]?

4. Don't get defensive.

5. Provide room for others to speak.

6. If it's a group portfolio critique session, avoid being over-enthusiastic about one portfolio and not another. Be consistent with praise.

If you are a facilitator for a group critique

1. Explain how the session will run.

2. Ensure portfolio owners provide sufficient context.

3. Encourage members of the group to share 1 or 2 pieces of feedback. If there is the risk of louder voices drowning out quieter ones, consider asking people to quietly write their feedback on sticky notes before a round of sharing.

4. Remind participants to be kind.

5. Keep track of time.

Should you ask for feedback if rejected for a role?

You won't always get feedback if you're rejected for a role, even if you attend an interview. And if you do receive feedback, it may not be that meaningful.

People tend to avoid giving feedback because:

- People don't like having potentially uncomfortable conversations.
- They're worried they could say the wrong thing and end up in legal trouble.
- They have better things to do than talk with someone that isn't being hired.

If you want to give asking for feedback a try, keep it positive and simple:

> "While I'm disappointed I wasn't chosen, I would appreciate the chance to get some honest feedback as I am still very interested in working with you in the future.
>
> If you could spare a few moments to drop me a few lines or have a conversation, I would be most grateful."

CLOSING WORDS

If I'm honest, I wrote this book out of frustration.

Whilst I'm tired of seeing people moan about having to create a portfolio or posts proclaiming that UX portfolios are the wrong tool, I'm more frustrated by the number of articles online that offer candidates bad, subjective advice about portfolio design.

Something evidence-based was sorely needed.

I hope this book fulfils this need and that it enables you to embrace the UX Portfolio and achieve what you want in work and life.

Good luck!

APPENDIX 1: PORTFOLIO PLANNER

This is a simple tool intended to help you plan the content and focus of your UX portfolio. To use it, follow these steps:

Review the job ad and other information from your target employer. Add what they are looking for to column one. In column two, write down your best project/activity examples that correspond to the needs listed in column one. In column three, list any artefacts, images, etc., that will serve as evidence.

Once you've listed everything your target employer needs, are there any items that seem more important than others? List these in column four. Consider mentioning these in your portfolio cover, introduction, or 'about me' content.

Review the projects listed in column two. Now write them into column five. Start with any projects in the same business sector. Otherwise, prioritise by frequency of mention. These projects are portfolio contenders, in the order you may wish to present them.

Place the key job requirements into column 1

PRODUCT DESIGNER

RESPONSIBILITIES

- Conceptual ideas into something useful and valuable for users
- Incredibly simple and elegant design flows and experiences
- Strategic decisions with product and executive team
- Give and solicit feedback from other designers
- Partner to oversee the user experience of a product from conception until launch

MINIMUM QUALIFICATIONS

- Communication skills
- Strategic product thinking and vision
- Building and shipping applications or software
- Examples of interaction design work
- End-to-end (hybrid UX and UI) product design
- Execute on visual and interaction details

Place repeated requirements into column 4. For example, these are all collaboration

USER RESEARCHER

RESPONSIBILITIES

- Work closely with product teams to identify research initiatives
- Design hypotheses and lead studies
- Generate actionable insights
- Qualitative methods
- Quantitative methods, such as surveys
- Work cross-functionally
- Communicate results

MINIMUM QUALIFICATIONS

- MS/PhD, human behaviour related field
- 3+ years experience in applied product research
- Qualitative and user-centred design methods
- Quantitative, behavioural analysis and statistical concepts
- Ask/answer product and user experience related questions
- Compelling communication

If you have an example of anything specific mentioned (like surveys here), be sure to put it into column 3

171

UX portfolio planner

v1.1 Copyright 2020 Chopstix Media Limited. Personal use only. https://uxportfolio.design

1 List the skills and experience your target employer require

2 Write down your best projects and activity that correspond

3 Add the best images/artifacts you can share as evidence.

4 List what is most important to the target employer

5 List the most referenced projects from column two.

1 — List the skills and experience your target employer require	2 — Write down your best projects and activity that correspond	3 — Add the best images/artifacts you can share as evidence.	4 — List what is most important to the target employer	5 — List the most referenced projects from column two.
Conceptual ideas into something useful	Together - sending a message	Wireflow diagram	Collaboration with others	Snupps
Incredibly simple/elegant design flows	Snupps - onboarding	Wireflow diagram	Product design strategy	BT
Strategic decisions with team	Snupps - team workshops	Photos of team workshop results	User interface and interaction design	Together
Give and solicit feedback from designers	Virgin Media - weekly peer review	Critique guidelines I drafted		
Partner to oversee UX throughout project	BT - buzz project	Overview of design process		
Communication skills	Snupps - presentation to CEO	Stakeholder presentation deck		
Strategic product thinking and vision	Snupps - presentation to CEO	Stakeholder presentation deck		
Building/shipping applications/software	BT - buzz project - social screens	User interface designs		
Interaction design examples	Snupps - add item screens	User interface designs		
End to end UX/UI product design	Snupps	Overview of design process		
Visual and interaction design details	Together - sending a message	User interface designs		

173

UX portfolio planner

v1.1 Copyright 2020 Chopstix Media, Limited. Personal use only. https://uxportfolio.design

1 List the skills and experience your target employer require

2 Write down your best projects and activity that correspond

3 Add the best images/artifacts you can share as evidence.

4 List what is most important to the target employer

5 List the most referenced projects from column two.

1	2	3	4	5
Work closely with product teams	DW/QRS - workshops etc.	Team workshop plans / minutes	Close cross-functional collaboration	
Identify research initiatives	PWP - research planning	Research plan	Leading research - qual and qualint	
Design hypothesis and lead studies	PWP - research planning	Research plan	Communication of findings	
Generate actionable insights	QRS - testing analysis and communication	Show and tell deck		
Qualitative methods	Home office - User testing	User testing plan		
Quantitative methods, inc. surveys	QRS - customer survey and analysis	Customer survey		QRS
Work cross-functionally	QRS - testing analysis and communication	Show and tell deck		
Communicate results	QRS - testing analysis and communication	Show and tell deck		
Qualitative & user-centred design methods	PWP - customer interview plan	Customer interviews		PWP
Quantitative, behavioural, statistical	QRS - customer survey and analysis	Customer survey analysis		Home office
Ask/answer product/UX questions	Home office - open office hours			
Compelling communication	QRS - testing analysis and communication	Show and tell deck		

APPENDIX 2:
THE CASE STUDY CANVAS

The Case Study Canvas is a simple tool intended to help with planning UX case studies. It isn't just about UX portfolios. It can also be used to help you get your story straight for interviews or to prepare a presentation of your work.

To use it, work through the boxes, thinking about your project or referring to your notes. Write terse summaries only. The canvas is not meant to be your case study, only the outline for it.

Preparing for interviews

Once completed, review and reflect on the dashboard content. Think about your prospective employer/client and the elements you wish to emphasise.

Presenting your work

Lead your slide deck with the results. Follow with the business problem, the project challenges and how you approached them. Illustrate your deck with the images and artefacts you listed.

Creating your UX portfolio

Use the outline you've written in the canvas as the basis for writing a case study, then edit it for accuracy, clarity, and brevity.

UX case study canvas

1. Case study title

a) Project type or sector

2. Business problem or goal

b) Platforms

3. Results/Testimonials

c) Date/Duration

d) Project framework

4. Challenges

5. Approach

e) Process overview

f) UX tools and methods

6. Highlights

7. Images and artefacts

UX case study canvas

1. Case study title
What's the name of this project? May include client name.

2. Business problem or goal
What were you asked to achieve for the business? Go to the root requirement. If they asked you redesign something, why? What were they hoping to fix or achieve?

3. Results/Testimonials
List what the project achieved. Ideally, this would be some form of metric that demonstrates that the business problem was solved, or the business goal achieved. If you have no metrics, use a testimonial.

4. Challenges
What were the challenges during this project?

5. Approach
How did you approach the challenges?

6. Highlights
A highlight is a specific aspect of the project you wish to share with hiring managers. List possible items here.

7. Images and artefacts
List the key images and artefacts that will support your case study.

a) Project type or sector
Ecommerce? Healthcare? Banking? Something else?

b) Platforms
List the delivery platforms for the project.

c) Date/Duration
Duration is best.

d) Project framework
Agile? Scrum?

e) Process overview
Provide a high-level summary.

f) UX tools and methods
List the tools and methods you used on this project.

UX case study canvas

1. Case study title
UX design for start-ups

2. Business problem or goal
Secure additional seed funding by delivering a user experience similar to that offered by Facebook, Instagram, and other social media tools.

3. Results/Testimonials
App launched to the Apple AppStore on time.

Users rated it 5/5.

iTunes named it a best productivity app.

$5 million of seed capital secured.

4. Challenges
My individual interviews with the project team revealed:

• I was the fourth UX designer at the company within two years.

• UX design was a bottleneck for development, holding up delivery.

• The outgoing UX designer would create three designs alone for each item of new functionality. The founder would then pick elements from each design.

• Sometimes, the designs would be difficult to achieve in code, leading to bugs.

As a result, the app, which was currently in Beta, offered a disjointed experience, lacking in flow.

5. Approach
First, I sat next to a developer and made immediate, tactical changes to improve the app's user experience.

Secondly, I organised a new way of working for the team:

• The design and development teams would design together in workshops. Sketches would then be pair-designed into a single pixel-perfect prototype solution, which would then be presented to the founder for approval before moving into development.

This new way of working ensured solutions were fully thought through and technically viable.

6. Highlights
Sketches, team in action, final designs.

7. Images and artefacts
Mentoring of design team, Lean UX process, 360 degree testimonials (Client, Peer, Team member)

a) Project type or sector
Start-up

b) Platforms
iPhone/iPad native app, Responsive web app

c) Date/Duration
6 months

d) Project framework
Lean UX, Kanban

e) Process overview
Sketching > Pair designing > Prototyping > Delivery > Evaluation

f) UX tools and methods
Stakeholder interviews	
Heuristic review	**Sketch**
Collaborative design	**Flinto**
Sketching	**AppSee**
Pair designing	
Prototyping	
Critique sessions	
Analytics review	

APPENDIX 3:
UX PORTFOLIO CHECKLIST

Based on my portfolio research with researchers, designers, recruiters, and hiring managers, I've created the following checklist.

UX Portfolio Design Checklist

Have you:

☐ Identified the reviewers of your portfolio and their needs in terms of candidate experience?

☐ Curated a selection of realistic projects that demonstrate comparable work experience?

☐ Respected any non-disclosure agreement and privacy laws such as GDPR?

☐ Written the introduction to your portfolio so that it clearly articulates your value?

☐ Written your biography to convey what you can do for the reviewer, relevant experience, and your pleasant working nature?

☐ Written case study titles to summarise each chosen project?

☐ Checked that each case study is free of misspellings, typos, and poor grammar?

☐ Ensured that your portfolio is easy to navigate with no unnecessary interaction required?

For each case study, have you:

☐ Summarised your overall design process and given essential details such as project duration?

☐ Put the client into context: who they are, and the business outcome they needed?

☐ Communicated your role and how you collaborated with others?

☐ Explained vital decisions and the thinking behind them?

☐ Presented an understanding of research and design activities, including when to use them?

☐ Explained the business impact of the project, next steps, and your key learnings?

☐ Structured the content so that it is quick to scan, with ample headings?

☐ Used relevant photographs, cut-away artefacts, and other visuals in preference to wordy blocks of text?

RESOURCES

For resources on UX portfolio design, please visit
https://uxportfolio.design/

ACKNOWLEDGEMENTS

Writing this book proved to be the hardest thing I have ever done. I was plagued with self-doubt and imposter syndrome throughout. Midway through, I was diagnosed as autistic, which explained some of my challenges. Eventually, after much experimentation, I have been able to finish it.

I thank everyone who patiently waited for the book, and I apologise to those who wondered why it was taking so long.

So many intelligent people contributed to this book by sharing their wisdom with me through presentations, blog posts, or, in most cases, one-to-one conversations.

I will inevitably miss somebody. If that is you, I'm sorry. You really do have my thanks.

Adam Polansky

Aislinn Treacy

Alberta Soranzo

Alex Morris

Amanda Stockwell

Amy Jackson

Andrew Matlock

Angel Brown

Ash Donaldson

Ben Sykes

Brad Merry

Candice Diemer

Craig Moser

Dave Malouf

Jane Austin

Jared Spool

Jesse Stehle

Jon Kolko

Jonty Sharples

Justin Dickinson

Ken Musgrave

Mark Thomas

Meg Rye

Nick Grantham

Sean Pook

David Travis

Erin Malone

Kim Goodwin

Lynn Teo

Adam Churchill

Adam Connor

Adam Polansky

Alan Cooper

Alex Ng

Alison Atvur

Alison Austin

Al Power

Adam Babajee-Pycroft

Adam Connor

Adam Polansky

Adrian Howard

Alan Colville

Alan Cooper

Alexander Livingstone

Tony Beshara

Zach Cosmic

Mary Wharmby

Michelle T. Chin

Nick Finck

Troy Parke

Alex Morris

Alisan Atvur

Alok Nandi

Amber Matthews

Ambz Roberts

Amy Silvers

Andrew Boyd

Andrew Mayfield

Andrew Wong

Andy Budd

Angel Anderson

Angela Colter

Angel Brown

Anja Maerz

Anna Dahlström

Anne Stevens

Annette Priest

Annie Drynan

Arianne Stiles

Ash Donaldson

Austin Govella

Barry Briggs

Ben Gilmore

Ben Sykes

Bill Scott 🖤

Birgit Geiberger Boersma

Bonny Colville-Hyde

Boon Yew Chew

Brandon Stephens

Brandon Ward

Brett Lutchman

Brian Durkin

Brian Sullivan

Bruno Figueiredo

Bruno Martins

Carl Myhill

Caroline Jarrett

Carolynn Stanford

Cathy Wang

Chui Chui Tan

Chris Atherton

Chris Bush

Chris Chandler

Chris Palle

Chris Risdon

Christopher McCann

Christopher Schmitt 🖤

Christopher Troy Sanchez

Clive K. Lavery

Colin Irwin

Cornelius Rachieru

Dan Brown

Daniel Szuc

Danny Hope

Dan Oliver

Dan Saffer

Dan Willis

Darren Kall

Dave Ellender

Dave Gray

David Cain

David Fiorito

David "Sheff" Barker

Deborah Edwards-Onoro

Debra Levin Gelman

Denise Chroninger-Philipsen

Derek Featherstone

Derren Hermann

Devon Young

Diarmad McNally

Diego Pulido

Dominic Winsor

Donna Spencer

Dug Falby

Eddie Rich

Edward Tufte

Eewei Chen

Eric Scheid

Elizabeth Buie

Elizabeth Chesters

Eliza Miller

Emma Boulton

Erik Dahl

Erin Casali

Eurydice Sophia Exintaris

Evgenia (Jenny) Grinblo

Fairoz Noor

Fergus Roche

Filip Florek

Filip Szymczak

Francis Rowland

Francois Jordaan

Frank Gaine

Fred Beecher

Gabi Moore

Gaby Prado

Gary Barber

Gavin Harris

Gavin McFarland

Georgia Rakusen

Gene Moy

Geoff Alday

Gerard Dolan

Gerry Gaffney

Gerry Gant

Gerry Scullion

Giles Colborne

Gilles Demarty

Grace Carey

Graham Beale

Graham McAllister

Grandin Donovan

Greg Nudelman

Harriet Wakelam

Harry Brignull

Hubert Anyzewski

Ian Smile

Indi Young

Ivan Alarcon

Jackson Fox

Jake Causby

James Chudley

James Kelway

James McQuarrie

Jane Pyle

Jan Jursa

Jan Srutek

Jason Bootle

Jason Crane

Jason Grant

Jason Mesut

Jay Morgan

Jay Rogers

Jeff Gothelf

Jennifer Strickland

Jeroen van Geel

Jessica Ivins

Jill Reed

Jim Kalbach

Jiri Jerabek

Joan Vermette

Jochen Wolters

Johanna Kollmann

Joe Sokohl

Jon Fisher

Jose Coronado

Joshua Seiden

Jo Wong

Julie DeBari

Julie (jb) Booth

Justin Valle ♥

Katarzyna Stawarz

Kate Rutter

Keith Instone

Kevin M. Hoffman

Kim Bieler

Kim Goodwin

KJ Bottomley

Lane Goldstone

Laura Creekmore

Leah Buley

Lennart Hennigs

Leonie Tame

Linda Gehard

Lisa Fraser

Lisa Rex

Lis Hubert

Liz Kessick

Lola Oyelayo-Pearson

Lorelei Brown

Lori Widelitz-Cavallucci

Louis Rosenfeld

Lucy Buykx

Lucy Spence

Marcin Treder

Mark Dalgarno

Marko Mrdjenovič

Mark Skinner

Martha Aldridge

Mary Nolan

Martin Godfrey

Matt Balara

Matthew Oliphant

Matthew Woods

Megan Laybourn

Michael Adcock

Michael Calleia

Michael Carvin

Michele Ide-Smith

Michele Marut

Mike Atherton

Mike Biggs

Miles Rochford

Monica Ferro

Natalia Sprogis

Natasha Norton

Nick Cochrane

Nick Grantham

Nic Price

Noreen Whysel

Oliver Lindberg

Patrick Chamberlin

Patrick Sansom

Paul Finan

Paul Norris

Pedro Fernandes

Peter Boersma

Peter Grierson

Peter Lambert

Peter Morville

Pete Williams

Phil Amour

Ren Pope

Renata Phillippi

Richard Caddick

Richard Hare

Rick Threlfall

Robert Fransgaard

Rob Sterry

Rob Whiting

Ross Chapman

Rupert Bowater 🖤

Russ Unger

Ryan Rumsey

Ryan Sayers

Saielle DaSilva

Samantha LeVan

Sam Barnes

Sami Niemelä

Samuel Mikel Bowles

Séamus Byrne

Sebastian Deterding

Sedef Gavaz

Shah Widjaja

Shari Bare

Silvia Calvet Martin

Simon Norris

Simon Thompson

Sarah Zama

Shah Widjaja

Shannon Parsons

Shereen Mann

Sibila Spalding

Sjors Timmer

Sophie Freiermuth

Spencer Turner

Stephen Anderson

Steve Baty

Stuart Church

Stuart Cruikshank

Stuart Seddon

Stu Collett

Sue Priore Fensore

Susan Dybbs

Susan Weinschenk

Steve Portigal

Tanya Ahmed

Tanya Rabourn

Tanya Snook

Theresa Neil

Tim Caynes

Tim Minor

Tim Ostler

Tom Greever

Tonia M. Bartz

Tori Breitling

Tyesha Snow

Tyler Tate

Valeska O'Leary

Veronica Erb

Vicky Teinaki

Virginia Cagwin

Wiesław Kotecki

William Barraclough

Windahl Finnigan

Yvonne Shek

Zack Naylor

I have tried hard to identify the original authors or creators of all third-party frameworks in this book. In some cases, I was unable to do so. I am happy to correct any omissions.

I would also like to thank everyone that bought a conference ticket, attended a talk, signed up for a webinar or course, purchased a portfolio template, or requested a portfolio review.

Without you, this book would never have been completed.

ABOUT THE AUTHOR

Ian Fenn is an award-winning 26-year veteran UX consultant with a solid reputation for exceeding project targets through intelligent and thoughtful interaction design.

Based in London, UK, Ian is an accomplished speaker, frequently invited to speak at design and UX conferences.

www.ingramcontent.com/pod-product-compliance
Lightning Source LLC
LaVergne TN
LVHW051333050326
832903LV00031B/3505